access to philosophy

ENVIRONMENTAL ETHICS

Joe Walker

Hodder &

A MEMBER OF THE HOD

Some other titles in the series:

Issues of Life and Death
Michael Wilcockson   ISBN 0 340 72488 9

Introduction to the New Testament
Kevin O'Donnell   ISBN 0 340 72490 0

Future titles in the series:

Religion and Science
Mel Thompson   ISBN 0 340 75771 X

Sex and Relationships
Michael Wilcockson   ISBN 0 340 72489 7

Acknowledgements

The author would like to thank Lorna and David for their tireless patience yet again. Thanks are also due to Joe and Annie Walker, Bill and Cathie Craik, and David and Irene Gillies for their support, encouragement and kindness over many years.

Orders: please contact Bookpoint Ltd, 130 Milton Park, Abingdon, Oxon OX14 4SB. Telephone: (44) 01235 827720. Fax: (44) 01235 400454. Lines are open from 9.00–6.00, Monday to Saturday, with a 24-hour message answering service. You can also order from our website www.hodderheadline.co.uk.

British Library Cataloguing in Publication Data
A catalogue for this title is available form the British Library

ISBN 0 340 75770 1

First published 2000
Impression number   10 9 8 7 6 5 4
Year   2006   2005   2004

Copyright © 2000 Joe Walker

Cover photo from Environmental Images

Typeset by Transet Limited, Coventry, England.
Printed in Great Britain for Hodder & Stoughton Educational, a division of Hodder Headline, 338 Euston Road, London NW1 3BH by
CPI Bath

Contents

Preface

To the Reader

Access books are written mainly for students studying for examinations at higher level, particularly GCE Advanced Subsidiary (AS) Level and Advanced (A) Level as well as the Scottish National Qualifications in RMPS at Intermediate 2 and Higher Levels.

To use this book most effectively, you should be aware of the following features.

- The first chapter is introductory and sets the scene for the material in the rest of the book.
- The final chapter draws everything together.
- The Contents list gives a breakdown of the main sections in each chapter.
- Each chapter sets out Key Issues to focus your attention on the important questions.
- Within each chapter, the material is broken down further into subheadings and bulletpoints to make it easier to use.
- The Key Words at the beginning of each chapter are for easy reference and to help you become more familiar with the technical language of the subject.
- There are suggestions for further reading at the end of each chapter.
- There is also a Summary list of the main points at the end of chapters. It can form the outline of your study notes on the topic. It is also a quick revision tool.
- There is also help with answering examination questions, and a list of typical questions is given. Do tackle the specimen questions, just planning your answers to some of them and writing others in full.

General advice on answering essay questions
Structured questions will tell you what to include. The following advice is for those questions which leave it to you to work out.

- The most important thing is to read the question carefully and work out what it really means. Make sure you understand all the words in the question.
- Gather the relevant information for answering the question. You will probably *not* need everything you know on the topic. Keep to what the question is asking.
- Organise your material by drawing up a plan of paragraphs. Make sure that each paragraph is relevant to the question. Include different views within your answer (most questions require arguments for and against).
- Start with an introduction which explains in your own words what the question is asking and defines any technical words. Work through your answer in your carefully planned paragraphs. Write a brief conclusion in which you sum up your answer to the question (without repeating everything in the essay).

1 Environmental Ethics

1 Introduction

KEY ISSUES
- Is there an environmental crisis?
- What is/should be the relationship between humans and the natural world?
- Does the way we see nature affect how we treat it?
- How does thinking about the environment vary between East and West?
- Can the Environment be given rights? What would these rights be? How would they be decided, based on what and by whom?
- How do various ethical traditions respond to the concept of the environment?

There can be no prescription, no set of rules, for living within Gaia. For each of our different actions there are only consequences.

James Lovelock

One of the major growth areas of study today is 'The Environment'. The apparently precarious state of our home planet is a regular feature of scientific and ethical discussion, and most people have an opinion on environmental issues, whether it's the state of the ozone layer or local litter. The human species appears to have considerable impact on the natural world. Many environmentalists argue that nature is a finely balanced system which can easily be put out of balance with negative consequences, most of which are unpredictable. This fine balance, they would argue, is seriously affected by the actions of humans on Earth The effects of these actions should make us examine our attitudes to, and relationships with, the natural world. After all, we depend upon it for our survival now and for the continued survival of the human species for generations to come.

Environmentalists claim that Earth is able to support life so well by reacting to changes in the natural system – of which human activities are a part. However, these activities are so varied and may cause change so rapidly, that the environment may not have enough time to make the necessary adjustments. This might lead to unfortunate consequences for life on Earth, including us. Others respond that the natural world is so vast that human activities make little difference to what happens, besides which, natural systems are so complex that we wouldn't know where to begin if we tried to interfere with them.

This section explores whether there is any problem to be dealt with, the development of environmental awareness, and the ways in which ethical positions respond to environmental issues.

2 Is there an environmental crisis?

a) Yes

Many texts in this area refer to 'the environmental crisis'.

> We have killed off nature – that world entirely independent of us which was here before we arrived and which encircled and supported our human society. There's still something out there though – if you look out of the window, there's probably a cloud. In the place of the old nature there rears up a new 'nature' of our making … each cubic metre of air, each square foot of soil is stamped indelibly with our crude imprint, our X.

> Bill McKibben, *The End of Nature,* p.88

The position taken is that human activity has negatively affected the natural cycles of life on Earth. The pace of this activity is such that the natural responses of the Earth are not able to keep up, and so 'emergency measures' appear to be taking place. These emergency measures are predicted to be harmful for life on Earth – for example global warming produces rises in sea level and therefore flooding in many parts of the world.

Nature works through a series of cycles. Air, water and nutrients are continually recycled following use. As these cycles occur, they can be slowed, halted, or otherwise interfered with, with potentially dire consequences. These cycles naturally balance themselves out through a system called biofeedback. On a planetary scale this means that any imbalance in one system will be cancelled out by a regulatory mechanism in another. This will return the system overall to a state of healthy equilibrium.

One example should illustrate. The amount of carbon in the atmosphere has a direct effect on the amount of solar heat trapped by the Earth. Too much carbon free in the atmosphere traps too much heat and so the Earth warms rapidly. The temperature conditions for life on Earth fit into a narrow band, which if exceeded may result in problems both for life and for the planet's regulatory system as a whole. Earth therefore has mechanisms which trap carbon and fix it so that it is subtracted from the atmosphere. These 'sinks', as they are known, are, for example, living organisms. As organisms grow they consume carbon in various ways and then store that carbon in their own biomass. The trapped carbon in these organisms remains fixed to an extent throughout the organism's life. Even at death, the carbon may be released only slowly as the organism decomposes. Some organisms may have their carbon components further fixed by fossilisation. The trapped carbon then becomes part of the rocks, stored below the surface. Now, should this carbon be released quickly – for example by the burning of fossil fuels

– the many millions of years it has taken for the carbon to be fixed is reversed in minutes as the carbon is released back into the atmosphere where it has been absent for millions of years. The atmosphere then has to compensate rapidly or suffer the negative effects.

Environmentalists will argue that the rapid proliferation of humans on Earth has had just such negative biofeedback consequences in a fairly short time. For example, coal (fixed carbon) has been burned at a furious rate since the industrial revolution just a century or so ago – so vast amounts of fixed carbon have been released in a very short time. Nature has been unable to respond to this quickly enough and the response has caused a warming of the atmosphere which may have harmful consequences for life on Earth – including us.

This is just one example of many. The argument is that nature can only cope with change gradually. Sudden change calls for more drastic measures which may have negative implications for the system as a whole.

b) No

> Environmentalists, who are surely on the right side of history are on the wrong side of the present, risking their credibility by proclaiming emergencies that do not exist. What some doctrinaire environmentalists wish were true for reasons of ideology has begun to obscure the view of what is actually true in 'the laboratory of nature'.
>
> Greg Easterbrook, *A Moment on the Earth*, p.xvi

The Earth experiences constant change. This has always been the case throughout Earth's history. This change is what drives the system. By definition it cannot be static. For example, some changes which we now regard as problems – like global warming for example – were actually beneficial for the development of life on Earth in the past. Human activities are elements of this change which nature will respond to effectively one way or another. Humans have tended recently to over-exaggerate their potential impact on natural systems. Natural systems will always recover from change, and will do so by adjusting the system to cope with the new conditions. This might have negative implications for humanity but there is not much we can do about this – besides, what right have we to assume that nature must somehow maintain the correct conditions for the continued existence of our own species?

90 per cent of the species which have ever lived on Earth no longer exist. Extinctions are simply natural – indeed there have been many periods in the history of life on Earth which have come close to the extinction of all forms of life. We should not conclude that the human species is therefore anything other than another of the species of life on Earth which makes a brief appearance then disappears – killed, so to speak, by its own hand. Nor would it make

sense to devote far too much time to ensuring that this does not happen. Such a feat is beyond human capabilities, even though we think that we are capable of anything. This means that there is not an environmental crisis of any kind, only another chapter in the ever-changing systems of nature, which will take its course largely regardless of our own actions. Should humans disappear entirely from the planet, 'nature' will barely bat an eyelid, and the cycle of life will continue just as before. There is no environmental crisis – to imagine so is just looking at nature through human spectacles and assuming that nature is for our benefit. Human actions have consequences which nature will 'judge'. The effect nature has on life on Earth will be a logical outcome of that 'judgment'. Nothing more.

c) Perhaps

The complexity of natural systems is such that making any firm statement on the possible or actual effects of any activity on the environment is difficult. No one can be sure what action might lead to what result. The study of the interrelationships in natural systems is still in its infancy, and even with the development of powerful technology, the complexity of predicting something like cloud development and formation is still beyond us, never mind the entire range of global weather systems. Not only can we not be sure that the environment is suffering or benefiting from particular actions, we can be even less sure of the likely outcomes of potential responses to those things we identify as problems. The science of how we manipulate – intentionally or otherwise – natural systems is very vague still, and so whether the environment is in a state of crisis is difficult to judge.

Also, for the ordinary person, the science of the environment is complex, and so to know how one's lifestyle should be altered – if at all – to treat the environment more favourably is very difficult. The complex scientific conflicting views about the issues involved all sound credible, but they can't all be accurate. Instead, most people have to develop their own general response to the environment, and to that we now turn.

3 Developing environmental awareness

Many environmentalists trace modern 'Green' lifestyles to the moment when the space programme gave us our first view of the Earth from space. Some conclude that it was at this point that we became fully aware of the fragility of our own planet. This, combined with increases in knowledge about the vastness and complexity of the universe made us all the more aware that life on this planet was special and so worthy of conservation.

However, perhaps humans have always had an awareness of their dependence on nature.

a) 'Primitive' culture

In most cultures, the development of rites and practices to ensure the placation of natural forces is a typical feature. Nature is powerful. Early cultures took the view that this power could not be controlled but could be honoured. In return for this honour, nature would look favourably upon human endeavours. Many cultures assumed that natural forces were spiritual forces. The aim of certain rites was to ensure that these spirits were kept happy so that the force they controlled would work in our favour and not against us. Elaborate rituals including sacrifices took place designed to appease nature.

Many early cultures assumed that the sun, moon and stars were gods. In particular the sun, which warmed the Earth and caused the crops to grow, was worshipped. The Earth itself was seen as a living force which had to be kept happy so as to continue to produce the food we need. Often the sun and the Earth were seen as in some kind of relationship, and this relationship ensured the fertility of the land. In the Northern hemisphere, it was believed, for example, that during winter, the life-forces of many elements of nature slept to await the sun's return in the spring, when the lengthening days would arouse these sleeping forces, and bring 'new life' to nature.

Also, natural forces like winds and lightning were seen as having personality – often considered the anger of the gods or of nature itself, and in their destructive power forces to be reckoned with.

The relationship was simple. Humans depended on nature, which was in some sense divine. By satisfying this divine entity, humans could ensure their own survival.

> They gave sacrifice to the East/The East said 'Give it to the West'/the West said 'Give it to God'/and God said 'Give it to the Earth, for Earth is senior.
>
> Idoma (African tribal) prayer

This became particularly important the more humans engaged in settled agriculture. Often the chief/king was considered responsible for ensuring the satisfaction of nature, and would be considered responsible for famine, drought or other natural disasters because these would be seen as the displeasure of nature for the king's lack of effort. One of the theories for example, about the collapse of the Maya civilisation, was that repeated failure of crops led people to doubt the efficacy of priestly rituals. This in turn led to the collapse of social order and thus to the collapse of the culture itself. It is now suggested that this time of environmental disaster was actually either the result of the El Niño weather phenomenon, geologic or volcanic activity. Similar fates befell Egyptian civilisation as the elaborate rituals to appease the gods failed to produce the desired results from the sacred river Nile.

b) Biblical attitudes

In the West, much of our environmental attitudes derive from a Biblical ethic towards the environment. The Judaeo-Christian tradition argued that nature itself was not a living force, but something under the control of one God (Yahweh). The shift of appeasement therefore moved from nature to a God in whose image humans were believed to have been created. All through the Biblical account of humanity's relationship with God, there is a constant tension between the worship of the creator and the created. The Israelites worship of the Golden Calf is an example of this tension.

Nature is regarded as the 'handmaid' of God who retains absolute control over it. However, this can mean that God uses nature either to reward or punish. For example, the flood story is seen as God using nature to respond to human wickedness, and famines are still seen in Biblical times as God's response to faithlessness. Nature is God's creation and therefore subject to his will. Nature provides so that humans may survive in relationship with God, and its benefits may be withdrawn or modified at any time as a result of any problem arising in this relationship. Some argue that this tradition merely changes the previous relationship of Nature and man into man-like God and man.

Many environmentalists and moral philosophers argue that this Judaeo-Christian tradition, and its view of nature, is one of the reasons why we are in an 'environmental crisis', and so it is to this we will briefly turn.

> According to the Dominant Western tradition, the natural world exists for the benefit of human beings. God gave human beings dominion over the natural world, and God does not care how we treat it. Human beings are the only morally important members of this world. Nature itself is of no intrinsic value, and the destruction of plants and animals cannot be sinful, unless by this destruction we harm human beings.
>
> P Singer, *Practical Ethics*, p.267–8

i) Creation

The Biblical view is that God created all that there is in the universe, God himself being without cause. This creation culminated in the creation of life on Earth, and in particular in humankind. Having created all of this, God entered into a covenant, or agreement, with it. It would worship him and in return he would sustain its existence. Humankind was given a special responsibility over the natural world, summed up in a concept which has been the subject of wide discussion:

ii) Dominion

In the Genesis creation story, humankind, in the shape of Adam, is given dominion over nature. The interpretation of this concept throughout the ages has led to varying attitudes towards the relationship between humans and the natural world. In summary this concept could mean:

- **Domination** – Nature exists for humankind's use as we see fit. Power over nature is to be understood as absolute. God's granting of dominion to humankind means that creation is for human use and therefore anything is possible. The implication of this view is clear – that nature can be treated however we please because it exists for our benefit, and for no other reason. God created it for us therefore we are free to treat it as we wish. Many today argue that such an understanding of the concept of dominion has been the problem – in that we see ourselves as the centre of the universe, and that all nature is there for our use. Such domination is unlikely to foster an attitude of respect and care, rather it is likely to produce careless and thoughtless treatment of the natural world. Thus treating dominion in this way gives us an over-inflated sense of our own importance with negative consequences for the rest of the natural world. In this model we see ourselves not as part of nature but as above it, bending it to our will. This results in an attitude not of cooperation but of subjugation, where nature is seen as something to be tamed for our use.

However, such a crass understanding of dominion is arguably no longer generally accepted in the Judaeo-Christian tradition, if indeed it ever was. Many would suggest rather that this concept implies the notion of:

- **Stewardship** – Many theologians argue that to interpret dominion as domination is wrong and never was the intention nor was it how things worked out in practice. Certainly humans are the peak of God's creation, but only in as much as they are considered to be the creatures whom God has selected to regulate the response of the natural world to its creator, God. The role of humans is therefore twofold. Firstly to care for and conserve the integrity of creation as God has made it – because it is his; and secondly, to act as the director of nature's obedience to God. The peak of creation is more correctly God. Nature exists for him, and it is the role of humanity to ensure that such a situation continues as it began. The Earth belongs to God. Humanity is endowed with the unique ability to be the caretaker of this property.

To support this view, it is clear that there are restrictions placed on humanity's use of the natural world. There is a strong argument for example that the early Genesis material argues for a vegetarian approach to life. Moreover, later on in the Biblical material there are restrictions not only on what may and may not be eaten, but also on the ways in which nature itself must be treated. For example, the Jubilee year restriction which requires that the land be allowed to rest every seven years. Some might argue that this is simply the legal codification of practicality, others that this demonstrates an absolute requirement on humankind to remember the needs of the natural world even as nature is used for human benefit. Whatever the interpretation, the suggestion is clear – humans are given stewardship of God's creation. So they must look after it and ensure its sustained existence in a way which is pleasing to God. The Earth, and the natural world therefore, are to be regarded as a gift which is to be cherished as well as used. Such an interpretation of the concept of dominion has led many contemporary theologians in the Judaeo-Christian tradition to adopt a very strong environmental ethic.

The final Biblical consideration which is of importance in understanding the development of an environmental ethic which draws upon the Judaeo-Christian tradition is the concept of:

iii) The Fall

Many will suggest that current theological thinking about the relationship between humanity and the natural world is very closely related to this Judaeo-Christian concept. Fundamentally this is the notion that the natural world is suffering the consequences of the disobedience of humanity at the beginning. God gives mankind the choice between worshipping him and putting humanity at the centre of the universe. According to the myth, humanity chooses to disobey God and go its own way. Consequently humankind is punished by being banished from the paradise which God had created for it. Also, the whole of creation is tainted by mankind's disobedience and its relationship with God is thrown into question. This Fall (from a mutually beneficial relationship with God) affects everything in nature. It is therefore the task of humankind from that moment on to try to re-establish the agreement between mankind and God. This will lead in itself to the restoration of the bond between God and the natural world.

There are many interpretations of the Fall. However most theologians agree that it represents the idea of an ideal relationship with God which becomes soured. When the full agreement between God and man is re-established the relationship between the created and the creator will return to its original paradise-like state. Biblical history outlines the repeated attempts of God to re-establish the terms of the original covenant between creation and God, through the agency of the human species.

Such views may lead to a variety of attitudes towards the environment – for example, that concern for environmental issues is secondary to putting right the relationship with God after which all else will follow. It can also lead to the view that putting right environmental problems is much bigger than just tinkering with recycling and conserving species – it requires a whole change in the attitude of humanity towards the being which is claimed to have created it. Many might argue that this concept has led to a view of nature which sees little scope for improvement without a theological response. It is probably true that this view has played a significant part in environmental thinking in the past – at least up to the period of the Renaissance.

c) The ethics of the East

While Western thinking has been dominated by the belief in a single, all-powerful God, and the relationship between that belief in God and the development of science and technology, thinking in the East has taken a rather different route.
The general view here is twofold:

● Firstly, nature and natural processes are seen as cyclical. Ages come and go, and universes are continually created and destroyed, either by the actions of gods or by simple laws of cause and effect. Many eastern traditions suggest that rather than a beginning, the universe goes through cycles of beginnings and endings, eternally.

> The Buddhist is able to look at the mirror of nature without attachment and with equanimity, discern the most profound truths. He can see the essence of transience in the rhythms of nature – the falling of flowers, the decaying of leaves and the changing of seasons.

> Padmasiri de Silva, *Dharma Gaia*, p.15

● These laws are the laws of karma. This means the sum total of all actions as well as the individual build up of actions throughout our lifetimes. In short, the state of the universe, and so planet Earth, at any one time is the direct result of the build up of positive and negative karma. The aim of course is to ensure that positive karma outweighs negative karma, so that a net result of the positive is possible. When this is the case, good will follow. The traditions of the East therefore tend to see natural disasters and the like as the results of the build up of negative karma in this and previous lives.

In practice, this means that eastern traditions have tended to stress the importance of good actions towards all living things, as well as 'the environment' more widely. In particular, living things are thought to be trying to maximise their own good karma build up, and so it is important not to interfere with this process where that is possible. This has led many eastern traditions to hold that all life is sacred and should be kept free from unnecessary harm. Perhaps the most extreme example of this is in the ancient Indian religion of Jainism. Jain monks wear masks so as not to accidentally breathe in a fly, therefore harming it. This concept is known as ahimsa – non-violence – and has profound implications for the treatment of nature. If you believe that all living things have an intrinsic value, then you will be particularly careful about how you treat them, especially as this treatment not only has implications for them but also for your own state of existence in this life and the next.

> The Earth, our Mother, is telling us to behave. All around, signs of nature's limitations abound ... By protecting the natural environment ... we show respect for Earth's human descendants ... as well as for the natural right to life of all Earth's living things.
>
> The Dalai Lama (exiled leader of Tibetan Buddhists)

It is often suggested that this eastern rationale for living is far more environmentally friendly than the rather domineering approach in the West, based on our freeing ourselves from a creator God. However, many might argue that in today's society, this far more environmentally sensitive approach remains nothing more than theory because in practice the reality is no different in the East than in the West. It is countered that this is because of the domination of the East, or rather the developing world by the developed world, which leads to traditional beliefs being ignored in favour of economic gain, and to this we will return in Chapter 4. However, the difference is clear, in the eastern tradition there remains a value attributed to nature which is probably similar to the value placed on nature in the West in pre-Christian times, when it was believed that the best results could be achieved by working with nature, rather than against it.

Eastern religions have recently begun to use their beliefs to engage in environmental protection. For example, not long ago, a hardwood forest in Thailand was ordained as a community of Buddhist monks. Bizarre as this may seem it did put an end to attempts to cut the forest down, because local people refused to allow these 'monks' to be killed. The concept of interconnectedness is important for many environmental thinkers – the idea that all life on Earth is linked and what you do to one thing has potential effects on another.

Many eastern ideas were incorporated into western thinking in the 1960s alongside a rising interest in the religions of the East. Many philosophers also began to draw upon what are thought of as eastern ideas on the interconnectedness of all things in their environmental thinking.

4 Ethical theories

Generally, ethics can be split into a number of theories, each of which adopts a different approach to the environment and issues related to it. For a full account of the history and approaches of the most commonly followed ethical traditions you should see the book in this series entitled, *Ethical Theory*. However, we will briefly examine how the major ethical theories respond to issues arising from the topic of the environment. Firstly, however, here's a reminder of the major ethical traditions.

a) Egoism

This theory takes the view that we will always behave in ways which are beneficial to us. This benefit might be direct or not, but it will always be the motivation for our actions. Of course the difficulty here is in prediction. The egoist, when faced with a variety of moral choices will have to weigh these up and choose the option which he thinks looks most likely to produce the benefit for himself. This means that egoists will vary over their moral choices even when faced with the same situation, because one person's prediction of what the likely results of a moral choice might be may well be different from another's. More than this, one egoist's benefit may be another's drawback – so individual preferences will become important too. Nevertheless, the general principle remains. The egoist will do what is in his best interests – often regardless of the interests of others – unless of course, their interests benefit the egoist! The philosopher Thomas Hobbes (1588–1679) is an example of an egoist. He argued that people make moral choices based on their own desire for personal benefit, safety and glory.

One practical example of this egoism is hedonism which is the view that people behave in certain ways in order to produce the greatest pleasure for themselves. The trouble with this is that pleasure is a difficult idea to pin down and can take many forms. Seeking pleasure could lead the hedonist to make very selfish moral choices or very selfless ones. It also depends upon how accurately the hedonist is able to predict the outcome of his own actions – in other words, how could he be sure that his choices will actually produce the greatest pleasure? A development of this form of hedonism is another of the important ethical traditions for consideration:

b) Utilitarianism

> Actions are right in proportion as they tend to promote happiness, wrong as they tend to produce the opposite of happiness.
>
> JS Mill, *Utilitarianism*

The philosopher Jeremy Bentham (1748–1832) claimed that:

> The greatest happiness of the greatest number is the foundation of morals and legislation.

> J Bentham, *The Commonplace Book*

His view was that something is more likely to be right if it benefits many people as opposed to just one person. This idea became formalised in the principle of the maximisation of the greatest pleasure, or 'happiness' for the greatest number. Of course the problem here remains:

● How do you predict the outcome of any action? Will it actually produce the desired effect of the greatest good for the greatest number?
● Who decides what pleasure or happiness is? One person's pleasure may be another's nightmare.
● If the good of the many outweighs the good of the one, does that justify ignoring that one person's needs? Could this lead to individuals being 'sacrificed' for the common good? Would that be acceptable?

The philosopher John Stuart Mill (1806–73) is the best known exponent of this theory. He went further than Bentham because he argued that utilitarianism requires that we consider fully the possible outcome of the action (Act Utilitarianism); the place of rules (Rule Utilitarianism) – for example, should certain rules always be adhered to because they almost always lead to the maximisation of happiness for the greatest number; and personal preferences (Preference Utilitarianism).

These theories are classical ethical positions; however, there are many other ways of making moral decisions, some of which will draw on elements of these two.

c) Altruism

In some ways this is the opposite of egoism. This approach takes the view that when making ethical decisions we should take into account the wants and needs of others before our own. The beauty of this approach is that if everyone did this then we would have our wants satisfied without any need for action on our part – someone else would always have our best interests in mind! Of course again, there are difficulties with deciding what someone else would wish in a given situation. My idea of pleasure might differ from someone else's, so what they thought was in my interest is actually the opposite. Again there are problems with prediction – how can I be sure that my action will actually produce benefit for the intended person? For example, I may give a beggar some money as an altruistic act, but what if that beggar uses that money to buy alcohol which he drinks himself to death with? Has my altruistic action backfired, should I have foreseen this, am I responsible? The notion of what is in people's best interests is a recurring theme in ethics and no less so in relation to the environment, which of course, is often unable to express 'its wishes'.

d) Situation ethics

This approach judges each situation on its own merits. There are no hard and fast rules – only the principle that your decision should produce some desired outcome, and that the likelihood of this outcome will be related to that situation and that situation alone. A good example of this might be that even if you consider killing to be wrong generally, you may accept it (and perhaps even do it) in a situation where your life is threatened. The benefit of this approach is that each situation is looked at as a new moral problem. Of course the drawback is that, with no fixed rules but only general principles to guide you, it is difficult to decide what is right in each situation. Also, one person's assessment of the situation might differ from another's, leading inevitably to moral conflicts. The opposite approach to this in many ways is:

e) Legalism

The legalist obeys the law whatever it says, because by so doing he can be sure that his moral decisions are the ones which society as a whole – as represented by its legal codes – would agree with. Of course the problem here is when the law might be wrong. For example, during the construction of the Newbury bypass, many people broke the law by occupying the woods which were to be destroyed to make way for the road. A legalist approach to ethical decision-making puts a lot of trust in those who both make and police a society's laws. To make matters more complex, environmental law is still in its infancy.

> When the treaty setting up the EC was signed in 1957, environmental degradation was not generally recognised as an important problem. As a result, no express provisions relating to the environment were included in the treaty. However, international awareness of environmental problems increased greatly in subsequent years … Since 1972 the EC has adopted five action programmes for the environment and hundreds of laws …
>
> Dorothy Gillies, *A Guide to EC Environmental Law*, p.10

Finally, many people base their ethical decisions, not on philosophical principles alone but also by adhering to the teachings of:

f) Religious authority

This might be the teachings of a holy book, the traditions of a religious faith as expressed in its practices or through its teachers past and present. It might also be the result of direct 'experience' where the follower believes that their moral decision has been made for them by their god, and all they have to do is accept it and carry it out. This is a complex area because it involves a wide range of elements which go to make up your ethical decisions. Those who adopt such an approach will argue that it is a question of sincerity and acceptance – trusting that the decision you make is the right one for the right reasons – an intelligent synthesis of personal beliefs and the feeling that certain actions should be carried out.

Before we go on to explore how these ethical traditions respond to the general notion of 'The Environment', we should remember that most of these theories and ethical approaches are based on the principles of what is good with respect to human life on Earth. It is arguable that it is only comparatively recently that the strands in these ethical approaches which relate to the natural world have been identified and developed. To date, most ethics has been in relation to human interaction, not the links between the human world and the world of nature more widely. In fact, it might be said that many of the adherents of some of these ethical theories might find the idea of attributing rights to the non-human world a little odd. So we will briefly turn to the question of whether or not nature can be thought of as having rights at all.

5 Does the environment have rights?

Ethical theories take different approaches to the natural world, at least in relation to the extent to which rights can be attributed to it. Modern environmentalists argue that the environment should be given rights, at least so that our treatment of it is regulated.

a) Relationships

Many ethical systems take the view that rights can only properly be given to things with which humans can enter into relationship. One of the most important difficulties with giving rights to the environment is that what makes up the environment is a combination of living and non-living things. Different combinations of these things may or may not be given rights depending upon the circumstances or nature of their combination.

i) Non-living material things

Probably most people agree that a stone cannot be considered to have rights. When we kick it along a street no one is likely to accuse us of abuse, nor are we likely to be prosecuted for taking a hammer to it. However, many might claim that when it comes to hacking a piece of rock off a mountain, that could be considered a different matter. One stone is one thing – a collection of stones which make up a dazzling mountainside another. The value of the thing relates to the way in which we interact with it. While it is unlikely that one could form an affection for a stone, one can form a sense of protective affection for a collection of stones which become a mountain. Moreover, perhaps there is a difference in degree between hacking a small piece of stone off a mountainside and reducing the mountain to rubble through quarrying. What constitutes a relationship therefore is not as clear as it seems at first. However, it is probably true to say that people can form relationships with non-living material things. The link between people and the land on which they live is often very strong. Protecting this land is sometimes something people are willing to die for. While we are probably unlikely to have the same relationship with the land as we do with our family, relationships are still possible. In this relationship 'the other' has value for us and therefore should be treated in a morally correct way. The relationship between the aboriginal peoples of Australia and the land is perhaps the best known exmaple of this. The value of a non-living thing may vary according to the way in which we find it, as well as how we intend to use it. In this way it has instrumental value for us, and therefore our treatment of it has significance. One could go even further, however, and argue that non-living things may have intrinsic value, irrespective of our relationship to them. More of that later.

ii) Non-living, 'non-material' things

Can the atmosphere have rights? Or the carbon cycle? This is more complex still and relates to what rights are intended to do. Rights are mostly given to things in order to preserve them in a state which either they would like to be kept in, or which we consider to be as close to their natural state as possible. Clearly the atmosphere, for example, cannot express a wish to be in any state in preference over another, and this is the dilemma. When we pollute that atmosphere for example, we change its state from one thing to another. We then have to decide if that change has resulted in a deterioration of the 'natural' state of what it was before. If it is then we can conclude that there has been, in some sense, an infringement of that thing's rights. This means that we have to make a judgment about the point at which such a change reaches the stage where we can reasonably conclude that rights have been infringed – and such a judgment is going to be open to different levels of interpretation. While it is very difficult to form a relationship with an atmosphere in the traditional sense, it may still be possible to be in relationship with the natural world – even if that simply refers to climate. For example, the way of life of many people around the world is often closely bound up with the climate in which they live. Their 'relationship' with the climate is part of what defines such people as who they are. Should that climate change, then such people may have to undergo a drastic, and perhaps quite sudden, change in their way of life.

iii) Non-human living things

For many the relationship between humans and other living things is clearer still. One can engage in relationship with animal life. Animals also form relationships among themselves irrespective of the existence of humans. Most ethical traditions would accept that other forms of life should be granted certain rights, though not to the same extent as humans. Some traditions consider the degree to which another living thing has sentience – in other words, the ability to think and be aware of its own past and present and also make informed judgements about future possibilities. Some animals can do this to a very high degree, whereas most plants cannot. However, most ethical traditions would grant living things rights, but would vary about the nature and scope of these rights. To some extent this is the least complex area of environmental ethics, and yet many might argue it is the one which has been most ignored.

If ethical decisions are made in relation to the importance of relationships it is clear that the environment allows the possibility of relationships of many kinds. None of our ethical decisions are made in a vacuum and have implications across a range of species and natural cycles.

b) Consequences

Many ethical decisions are based on the likely consequences of certain actions. As far as the environment is concerned, this is often one of the strongest arguments used in any moral conflict. Actions have effects on other things. When we decide to do X instead of Y we know that there is a possibility that different consequences will occur. Generally, we want the consequences to be in some way favourable – but there's the problem. How do we predict what consequences will arise from what action, and how do we decide in the first place what the desirable consequences should be? This becomes especially difficult in relation to the environment because of the unpredictability of action and outcome. For example, the building of a dam may flood great areas of natural beauty and destroy many species, but the dam will provide work for many and perhaps a better standard of living for those who will benefit from the electricity produced. Building the dam will have a range of consequences. The difficulty is in weighing up these consequences. This involves giving value to some things more than others, and also valuing some outcomes more than others. The potential for conflict should be obvious, yet it is incredible how many in such situations still view the issues as 'black and white'. When taking consequences into account we already make value judgements before we begin and then at many other stages along the way. This giving of value is complicated by the dual nature of value itself.

c) Intrinsic value *v* instrumental value

The value of something may come from within itself (intrinsic) or in relation to its usefulness to other things outside itself (instrumental). Some environmentalists, known as 'Deep Ecologists', argue that nature has its own worth, unrelated to its usefulness for humankind. A species therefore should be protected for its own sake, not because it is useful to us. This approach means that the environment deserves preservation because it has its own value. This may not be able to be measured, or even appreciated by us but nevertheless it is still there. Put simply, the value of a chimpanzee can only ever be measured in chimpanzee. We cannot try to apply human rules of worth because they might not be appropriate in that case. Deep ecologists argue that just as we usually believe that human life is special because it is human, the environment should be regarded as special because of what it is. Imagine for example, that the aliens arrived and wanted to take away half the human population of Earth to their galactic zoo. How might we argue against this crime? Would we? Based on what? The problem with this is that when you regard everything as having intrinsic value, how does this affect your actions towards it? A simple example: all humans need to eat other living things in order to survive. If all life on Earth has its own intrinsic value, then unfortunately we will have to violate that value in some way at some time. This makes the idea of intrinsic value of all elements which go to make up the environment a difficult idea to hold on to if we are going to live 'normal' lives.

Another way of looking at something's value is in terms of its instrumental value. This means that the value of a thing is tied partly or completely to its usefulness for some purpose or other. As far as the environment is concerned many people take this approach. If we harm the environment then the negative consequences for the future of human life on Earth might not be so good, therefore it is in our own interests to look after the natural world. Seen this way, nature is regarded simply as something which we need to keep us alive, which we should protect for our own benefit. It has no value in itself, just usefulness for us. The problem with looking at things this way is that it seems quite cold and calculating. Imagine, for example, your house was on fire. You were being visited by a world famous scientist who is close to discovering the cure for cancer. The fire brigade know this and decide to save him first leaving you exposed to the flames. While you might appreciate that the scientist now has more immediate instrumental value than you, it won't make you feel any better about going up in flames. An additional problem is this: instrumental value is often difficult to judge – for example, imagine that this scientist was losing his memory, and was in the middle of giving you all the information he had gained till now in his cancer research. In fact (if you could see into the future) he was never going to discover the cure for cancer – you are.

d) Absolute *v* relative rights

If you take the deep ecologists' approach then you have to give absolute rights to the environment and all its components. The problem with absolute rights is that they do not allow for variety in the situation. For example, if you believed that it was the absolute right of all living things to be free from harm, then you would have to find a new foodsource for the human species. More than that, however, if the right to life is absolute, how would you respond to instances in nature where one living thing takes the life of another? Obviously it would make little sense to prosecute the lion for killing its prey, because that is what it needs to do to survive. However, where does this approach leave vegetarianism? We need to eat to survive so we cannot be criticised for some amount of killing, and thus depriving other living things of their absolute rights. There are people who take absolute rights seriously – for example never killing, nor even taking what is not given. For example, Buddhism teaches that there are absolute rights to life, but that inevitably, this will be unavoidably broken many times throughout our lives. The way to get over this is to take into account that when rights are infringed, if this is done with the right intention, then the infringer – while not getting off the hook entirely – at least limits the damage done as far as possible. We will return to this idea later.

The solution for many is to consider that rights are relative not absolute. What they are relative to differs widely, according to your ethical perspective, but the idea is simple. Rights can be infringed in certain circumstances. The best example of this idea of rights as relative is war. All societies include prohibitions in their laws about the taking of human life. In most societies it is considered the ultimate crime and appropriately punished. However, during a war we give people the right to override this rule so that they can kill 'the enemy' and so protect us from possible harm. In this way it is clear that human life cannot be thought of as an absolute right, but as a relative one – a right which can be suspended if the situation requires it. As far as the environment is concerned this presents us with problems. Who decides when rights should be suspended? Based on what? Most agree that a beautiful forest has a 'right to life' – but what if that forest's continued existence stands in the way of 'progress'?

6 Ethics and the environment

Before we look at specific environmental issues in the following chapters, we will summarise responses of the ethical traditions mentioned previously in relation to the rights and treatment of 'The Environment'.

a) Egoism

- If use of the environment helps me maximise my pleasure then that is morally acceptable;
- Where treating the environment in a certain way will cause me pain or suffering, then that treatment should be avoided;
- The environment only has rights when those rights can lead to the maximisation of my pleasure;
- The environment therefore can only have rights in as much as these rights benefit me – the environment has only limited rights;
- The environment can be treated in any way which brings me benefit;
- Therefore the accurate prediction of the likely outcome of any course of action is important because getting it right will affect my pleasure.

b) Utilitarianism

- The use of the environment must produce the greatest benefit to the greatest number at the least 'expense';
- Pain and suffering resulting from the treatment of the environment is acceptable provided that this results in the most benefit for the greatest number;
- The environment has rights only when those rights lead to the maximisation of benefit for the greatest number;
- Treatment of the environment must therefore result in a balance of pleasure over pain for the many – even if this is at the expense of the few, or of non-human things;
- The environment has only limited rights where these rights do not infringe the benefit of the many;
- The prediction of the likely outcome of any course of action is important so as to balance out accurately benefits and drawbacks.

c) Altruism

- The use of the environment must produce the greatest benefit for others;

Moral stance	How should environment be 'treated'?	What rights should the environment have?	Problems
Egoism	As you like provided it is in your own interest	Only those rights which you think will result in personal benefit	● predicting cause & effect difficult – what is likely to produce most personal benefit? ● others may suffer for your self-interest
Utilitarianism	For the benefit of the majority	Only where such rights can be seen to benefit the majority	● minority interests may suffer ● why should nature exist for people?
Altruism	In a way which produces benefits for others	Only when such rights produce benefits for others	● you may have to make many personal sacrifices ● predicings 'costs' & 'benefits' is difficult
Situation Ethics	According to the needs (perceived) of an individual situation	Varies as a function of changing situations	● no consistency of approach ● accurate & reliable assessment of each situation required
Legalism	According to the rule of law	Idea of 'rights' for environment still developing. Currently a composite idea based on many legal sources.	● Variations between nations' laws causes complexity ● laws may be vague or ethically unacceptable

Figure 2 – Summary chart of the five moral stances

- Pain and suffering resulting from the treatment of the environment is acceptable provided that this results in benefit for others;
- The environment has rights only when those rights lead to the maximisation of benefit for others;
- Treatment of the environment must therefore result in a balance of pleasure over pain for others – even if this is at the expense of non-human things, or even me;
- The environment has only limited rights where these rights do not infringe the benefit of others;
- The prediction of the likely outcome of any course of action is important so as to balance out accurately benefits and drawbacks so that other people obtain the greatest benefit.

d) Situation Ethics

- Treatment of the environment is to be decided based on each situation as it arises;
- Given that no two situations are the same, it would be difficult to ascribe absolute rights to the environment;
- Each individual or society must therefore make ethical decisions about the environment by looking closely at the range of benefits and drawbacks of each situation;
- The rights of the environment in relation to people may be greater or less depending upon the situation;
- Therefore accurate assessment of the facts, opinions and likely outcomes of any action is important.

e) Legalism

- The rule of law in relation to the treatment and rights of the environment should be followed;
- In relation to environmental issues in one country, responses to this should take into account: the law of that country, natural law, as well as international law;
- The environment could therefore be ascribed rights by society which could be enshrined in law;
- Once these rights were made law, they could not be altered without 'due process'.

7 Conclusion

You should be aware that there are many different ethical approaches to environmental issues, and you should be able to respond from any of these positions, as well as criticise them when required. You should also be aware that moral issues are by their nature complicated and subject to conflict. You should not only be able to demonstrate an awareness of that conflict but also show that you can enter into it and reach your own thought-out conclusions. Most importantly perhaps – and certainly for what follows in the next chapters – you should be aware that environmental issues are not only complicated ethically, but in many other ways too, for example politically and scientifically. The environment as a topic produces very passionate responses across a range of groups and individuals. As an example, you may be aware that a Greenpeace ship was bombed in New Zealand some years ago, resulting in deaths. Even today many environmental protesters find themselves regularly imprisoned. To be able to make informed comments about the rights and wrongs involved in environmental issues you should know your facts and know how to analyse them properly.

Study guides

Summary List

You should build your study notes on the following:

- What constitutes the environment?
- To what extent is the environment in a state of crisis today?
- How has public awareness of the environment developed over time?
- How has the Christian faith influenced thinking about the environment in the West?
- How has this thinking been affected by the development of modern science?
- Can the environment have rights?
- What might these rights be, what are they based on and who grants them?
- What is/should be the relationship between the human species and the rest of the natural world?
- What general ethical theories are adopted by thinkers in the western world?
- How do these theories each approach the idea of rights for the environment?
- Which of the ethical theories do you think is the most helpful for the environment?

Examination Guide

Questions in this area are likely to ask you to do the following:

- demonstrate awareness of the variety of environmental issues today;
- show that you understand the development of thinking about the

environment with time;
- outline and analyse ethical responses to the concept of the rights of the environment;
- develop and support your own conclusions about the scope and extent of rights for the environment;
- demonstrate that you understand the complexity of the arguments involved but that you can also arrive at your own reasoned conclusion.

The skill will be not just to show that you know your material, but that you also have command of it. This means for example, that you should not just know what utilitarianism is in general, but you should be able to apply its theory to the specific environmental issue raised.

Also, you should try to show in this general section that you have a good knowledge of current affairs related to the environment (and who knows what environmental issues will be in the news by the time you read this). You should be able to refer to these and work them into your general ethical arguments where possible.

What you must guard against – particularly if you have strong feelings about the environment – is setting these feelings out in an emotive way without reason and support. The examiner is not there to judge your opinion, but to assess how well you can express your opinion and use what you have learned to support it. He may also want to see that you can argue a point from a stance which is not your own. This will be more difficult if you are determined only to set out your own views. That is not to say that you should not argue passionately about something which you believe – just remember not to be too narrow in your responses, and to remain cool and objective in your statements.

Sample Essay Question Guide

'It makes no sense to give rights to the environment – such a 'thing' does not really exist.' Discuss.

1. Outline your own assessment of what actually constitutes the environment. You should include information and viewpoints which highlight the complexity of pinning down the environment as a concept.
2. You may like to explore to some extent the historical development of the concept of the environment. This will show that you are aware of how the relationship between the human species and the natural world has changed with time. This should also show the extent to which the environment can be thought of as a thing.
3. You should discuss the concept of rights. How do we decide what should and should not have rights? Who makes these decisions and what are they based on? In what ways might it not be sensible to give the environment rights and in what ways is the opposite true? Perhaps you should set out the rationale for giving things rights generally.

4. You may like to take a couple of the moral stances and show how these might respond to the idea of giving rights to the environment. In this section you should show how rights, or the lack of them, for the natural world would affect the basic premise of these ethical traditions and their thinking. In other words, for example, how might a hedonist be affected by living in a natural world which had rights of its own?

5. Finally, in a discussion question you should aim to give at least two opposing viewpoints in relation to the statement, one supporting it and one rejecting it. Remember to analyse each point of view as you go along, but do not forget to include your own conclusion. You should briefly draw all your writing together in order to answer the question from your own point of view. In the case of this question the final section of your essay should begin something like this:

It makes perfect sense to give rights to the environment because …

OR

It makes no sense to give rights to the environment because …

OR

In some ways it makes sense to give rights to the environment, and yet in other ways it does not because …

In this concluding section you should give full supporting reasons for your point of view. You can either express it as your own viewpoint or merely your own assessment of the viewpoints you have previously covered during the main part of your essay. It is always good practice in an essay to use the actual wording of the essay question within the essay. If nothing else, it helps remind you regularly what the essay is about.

Typical Examination Questions

1. 'The present environmental crisis is largely the fault of the human species.' Discuss

2. 'Humans have only recently become aware of the needs of the natural world.' To what extent is this statement accurate?

3. To what extent has the concept of 'Dominion' affected the human view of the environment?

4. 'Darwin's evolutionary theory means that humans feel no need to exercise concern for the environment because the theory shows that change is a necessary feature of the cycles of nature.' How might an environmentalist argue against this position?

5. 'The building of a dam involves a great many ethical conflicts.' Discuss

6. How might a utilitarian respond to an invitation to join an organisation such as Greenpeace?

7. To what extent should our treatment of the natural world be concerned only with the consequences of our actions?

Activities

In this introductory section, role plays based on areas of environmental conflict will allow you to develop your thinking about how ethical responses approach environmental issues. You will get further practice in this during the following chapters as we consider specific environmental issues. However, for the moment here is one kind of exercise to try out:

> The scene is a court. A major dam project is about to be undertaken. Country X's government is supporting the dam and environmentalists oppose it. Work though the court case in your class. Try where possible to have arguments which draw upon some of the ethical theories you have studied. For example, give each 'witness' an ethical theory to draw upon during their submission to the court.

Suggestions for Further Reading

1 *Ethics*: Mel Thompson; Hodder & Stoughton, 1994,
  ISBN 0 340 61101 4
2 *Ethical Theory*: Mel Thompson; Hodder & Stoughton, 1999,
  ISBN 0 340 72075 1
3 *Green Christianity*: Tim Cooper; Spire, 1990, ISBN 0 340 52339 5
4 *Gaia: A New Look at Life on Earth*: JE Lovelock; OUP, 1987,
  ISBN 0 19 286030 5
5 *The End of Nature*: B McKibben; Penguin, 1990, ISBN 0 14 012306 7
6 *A Moment on the Earth*: G Easterbrook; Penguin, 1995,
  ISBN 0 14 015451 5
7 *Practical Ethics*: P Singer; Cambridge, 1993, ISBN 0 521 43971 X
8 *Dharma Gaia*: AH Badiner (Ed); Parallax Press, 1990,
  ISBN 0 983077 30 9
9 *A Guide to EC Environmental Law*: D Gillies; Earthscan, 1999,
  ISBN 1 85383 585 4

2 Specific Environmental Issues

KEYWORDS

biodegradeable – where material can break down safely in a natural environment after disposal

climate – the regulatory systems of the Earth which include the weather, the internal processes of the Earth as well as the interrelationship between living and non-living things on the planet. Works on a system of feedback

fossil fuels – the use of fossilised organic matter as a fuel liberates stored carbon into the atmosphere which then combines to produce CO_2, a greenhouse gas

global warming – the theory that the Earth's climatic temperature is rising with negative consequences for life on Earth. Many argue that this change brought about by human activity. Principally referred to as the Greenhouse Effect

ozone layer – a layer of the atmosphere which filters the sun's U-V radiation. Consists of molecules of O_3

pollution – the introduction of abnormal substances into a given environment, or substances which though not abnormal are in such concentrations as to cause harm to the overall system

sustainable – where the use of something can take place without detrimental effects to its future use or supply. Usually applied to energy production and resource depletion

1 Introduction

KEY ISSUES
- What environmental issues face us today?
- What are the possible causes and effects of these problems?
- How far do humans contribute to environmental problems?
- To what extent are there differences of opinion about how to deal with environmental problems?
- How do various ethical traditions respond to the issues raised?

'Think Globally, Act Locally'

Friends of the Earth slogan

Perhaps one of the most significant difficulties with environmental issues is the range of disciplines they involve. For each environmental issue there are scientific, political, social, economic and behavioural dimensions. This makes the specific issues which this chapter will explore very complex. There is also the problem of access to objective information – environmental issues tend to force people to take sides, and when this happens, those people use the information which best suits their point of view. Some might argue, for example, that an oil company is hardly likely to support scientific research which reaches the conclusion that drilling for oil is very bad for the environment. In fact, it is likely to do the opposite: sponsor research by other scientists who do not agree that drilling is harmful. Similarly, any scientist who suggests that the greenhouse effect does not exist is likely to face opostition from environmental groups. Getting hold of balanced and reliable information on some topics is therefore very difficult. There are many vested interests in environmental issues, and you should be aware of this when reading materials on the topics.

Besides this, many of the topics are genuinely inconclusive. Every time some scientist provides evidence which suggests that global warming is caused by human activity, another scientist provides evidence that it is not. The science is complex, and often leaves members of the public very unsure about whether there is any environmental crisis or not.

Also, even if every scientist in the world agreed tomorrow that human activities are causing a hole in the ozone layer, they would not all agree about how to deal with it. And that's just the science – there would then have to be political and economic decisions taken by the world's governments. As you might expect, there might be differences of opinion here. Even at the level of the individual there would have to be choices made. Not everyone might agree that certain actions are necessary, some may not want to change their ways – or may not be able to.

The decisions that we make will also be informed by our personal ethical philosophies. You have seen in the first chapter how these relate to the environment generally, now we will try to apply them to specific issues.

This chapter will look at three specific areas:

- climate change
- pollution
- the use of the Earth's resources

For each of the issues in these general sections we will explore the background information, the scientific and political implications of the issue itself, the extent to which it is a problem, and the responses of the ethical traditions to the specific issues raised.

2 Climate change

It is generally agreed that the Earth's regulatory systems are finely balanced. Any alteration to that balance will require a response mechanism which will return the system to equilibrium. The climate is perhaps the best example of the complexity of this balance. The Earth's climate sustains life – but only certain kinds of life within certain fairly narrow bands of climate. Change the climate and you change the possible life-forms. Most of the previous extinctions of life on Earth were the result of climate change. Climate change can be rapid. The ability of living things to respond appropriately to it is not. Without adaptation a species dies. It is widely argued therefore that if we want to maintain life on Earth as it is at the moment, then we have somehow to ensure that climate change is not too drastic nor too rapid. It is further argued that the activities of humans in the recent past have had a seriously negative effect on the Earth's climate. If these activities go on unchecked, then the implications for life on Earth as we know it could be serious. Currently the most clearly identified potential problems for the Earth's climate are the possibility of global warming and the destruction of the Earth's ozone layer.

a) Global warming

i) The greenhouse effect – an explanation

> … the greenhouse age may turn out very differently from that predicted by the climate modellers. Change may come suddenly, rather than slowly over decades. There may be utterly unexpected developments … Most worrying of all, the greenhouse could trigger changes in the oceans or forests that escalate the greenhouse effect …
>
> F Pearce, *Turning up the Heat*, p.11

Most of the 'heat' which we experience on Earth is the result of solar radiation. The Sun is effectively a massive nuclear reactor with a surface temperature around 6000°C. It emits radiation which travels through Space and arrives at Earth in the form of heat, light and electro-magnetism. This is the Earth's principle source of energy, without which life as we know it would not exist. Solar radiation arrives at different wavelengths. When this reaches Earth a variety of things may happen to it:

- some is directly reflected back into space by the Earth's atmosphere
- some is reflected by clouds into the atmosphere
- some is reflected by the Earth's surface including the oceans
- some is absorbed by the Earth and the oceans and re-emitted into the atmosphere at different wavelengths
- some is directly absorbed by the atmosphere.

If the Earth had no atmosphere then this solar radiation would behave quite differently, and the Earth would be a different place. However, the atmosphere effectively traps a considerable amount of this solar energy and stores it as heat. Just as the glass in a greenhouse lets through the short-wave radiation of the Sun and traps the long-wave, thus heating the greenhouse, the Earth's atmosphere works in similar ways. This is a natural process, without which life on Earth would have taken a completely different evolutionary route.

What is at issue is the amount of solar radiation which the Earth's atmosphere traps. It must retain some of the heat, but not too much, because if it does then the climate overall will warm up with potentially harmful consequences.

The heat is trapped by certain gases present in the atmosphere. These have become known as greenhouse gases, and it is the sources of these greenhouse gases which has become the major feature in disagreements over this environmental issue. The major greenhouse gases are:

- Carbon Dioxide (CO_2) – arguably the principle greenhouse gas, this is a by-product of many biological functions, including respiration and photosynthesis. It is also released during the decay of biological organisms which contain carbon, as well as the weathering of inorganic materials which contain carbon, as well as many other Earth processes including volcanic and geothermal activity.
- Water Vapour (H_2O) – again, a by-product of natural processes on or in the Earth.
- Methane (CH_4) – the by-product of anaerobic respiration, digestive processes and decomposition.
- Ozone (O_3) – poisonous to life in the lower atmosphere. This gas is produce by a photochemical reaction with other gases in the atmosphere.
- Nitrous Oxide (N_2O) – another gas which results from natural biological processes.

All of these gases are present in the atmosphere naturally, and are involved in an intricate system of balance where their relative abundance is kept stable by atmospheric processes – that is, until their concentrations in the atmosphere are raised quickly and/or significantly.

Should this happen then the climate will warm up – it may do so only very slightly though this may be enough to trigger some fairly significant results:

ii) The greenhouse effect – possible effects

- There could be fairly significant changes to weather patterns on Earth, particularly in relation to the water cycle. Some places may become much drier and some much wetter. This change in weather systems might also produce much more of what we consider to be 'freak' weather. Even where this does not occur, changes to the pattern of global weather systems will affect the growth of plants and therefore the food chain itself of which plants are the base. This global warming could, in short, produce climatic imbalance which could have direct or indirect implications for the stability of life on Earth. Such changes to the climate would have a direct effect on humans, because it would result in significant changes to the pattern of agriculture. This would have economic implications – as countries have to adjust to their new agricultural limitations or possibilities – but it could also have political implications. For example, fresh water supplies could be altered. This could lead to international conflicts.

A warming of the atmosphere may also produce significant rises in sea-level. This could happen because as the sea itself warms it expands and rises, but it could also happen as the store of frozen water on the Earth is melted. Glaciers, ice sheets and the polar ice-caps contain a great deal of water in a frozen state. Were this to melt then it could result in rises in sea level. This would have direct effects, because a considerable proportion of Earth's population lives at coastal margins. These populations would require to migrate to higher land, and the infrastructure they had lived with would have to be re-built. Some low-lying countries, like many coral atolls in the pacific, might disappear entirely. As sea-levels rose, not only would many areas of land be flooded, but land which had been used for agriculture could now be unusable. Just a one-metre rise in sea-level might take almost a third of the Earth's productive agricultural land completely out of use.

The most significant feature of the effects of global warming are twofold. Firstly the effects of global warming will extend to all life on Earth as well as the Earth's regulatory processes themselves. All species – not just humans – will experience a change in their environment and will have to adapt as best they can. Secondly, the effects are unpredictable. Any predictions are educated guesses because the systems we are dealing with are so complex. There may actually be benefits to be had from global warming as well as drawbacks, no one knows for sure, and that is part of the problem. What is certain is that a runaway greenhouse effect is unlikely to be helpful for life on Earth, and particularly so for the human species.

While no one knows exactly how, when or indeed if global warming will occur – or what the exact consequences are likely to be – the present environmental debate centres on this: How far are human activities accelerating this natural process beyond the ability of the Earth's regulatory systems to cope with it? Or is it just a natural occurrence?

iii) The greenhouse effect – a natural cyclical process
Whether or not there is or could be a greenhouse effect is open to debate. This is partially because of the complexity of the climate, but

also because there are other possible factors which might cause such an effect:

- Geological activity – the Earth traps and releases the substances which cause greenhouse gases naturally. Sometimes this happens slowly, such as the weathering of carbon-based rocks, or suddenly, as in volcanic eruptions which put out vast amounts of solar radiation-trapping gases at any one time. These events may also change cloud structure, thus changing the albedo (reflective capacity) of the atmosphere which may warm up, or cool, the planet.
- Natural climate cycles – the Earth's climate is not entirely stable. Ice ages have come and gone, changing the atmosphere completely for a period of time. The cause of these is not clear but they may happen because of changes in the Sun's activity, wobbles in the Earth's orbit or spin on its axis. Tectonic activity may also cause these including Earthquakes and movements of land. For example, when the Indian sub-continent crashed into Asia many millions of years ago, the force of the collision pushed up the land to the north. This created the Tibetan plateau. Many scientists believe that this change in the landscape produced changes in the airflow around the Earth, resulting in climate change and producing an ice-age. During ice-ages, ice sheets come and go, either reflecting more or less solar radiation.

These explanations apart, it is widely agreed that human contributions to a possible greenhouse effect are significant and do require our attention.

iv) The greenhouse effect – the human connection

So far as the climate is concerned, at this stage planning is as far as we are able to go. So far as the wider global environment is concerned we can go further, and perhaps we should; for regardless of what may happen climatically, there are appropriate reforms we might make whose outcome would be a cleaner, healthier and more equitable world.

M Allaby, *Living in the Greenhouse*, p.188

Most greenhouse gases occur perfectly naturally as the by-products of natural processes on Earth. In what ways might human activities increase the concentrations of these gases?

- CO_2 – Carbon stored in living organisms is released when those organisms are destroyed, forming CO_2. The vast majority of fuel used by humans is carbon-based. As this material is burned (oxidised), the carbon which it holds is released increasing the CO_2 concentrations in the atmosphere. The burning of fossil fuels is of particular concern. The use of such fuels represents the liberation of carbon which has been stored for millions of years. Coal, oil and gas are all fossil fuels, and the world's economy is based upon these products. The combustion of fossil fuels is widely considered to be the main way in which humans may contribute to the greenhouse effect. CO_2 is also released when organic matter is destroyed. One of the main ways in which humans can cause this is by the destruction of forest areas. As this occurs, the carbon stored in the wood and plants decays giving off CO_2. This is made worse where forest is cleared for agriculture, because this usually means burning the forests which liberates the carbon very quickly. To make matters worse, the removal of the forest withdraws one of the ways in which the Earth would otherwise remove CO_2 from the atmosphere. So more is added and less is able to be removed – a double blow.

- N_2O – This is also released as plant material is burned, so when proteinous material is used as fuel or burned to clear for agriculture, N_2O is released. Also, modern agricultural practice involves the heavy use of nitrogenous fertiliser. Much of this nitrogen finds its way into the atmosphere.
- CH_4 – The principle source for this gas is the digestive processes of agricultural livestock – in particular cattle. It is also produced as a result of the process of growing rice. As fields are drained, bacteria release considerable quantities of the gas. Small amounts of methane also come from mining operations and as the result of the decomposition of matter in landfill sites. One of the greatest contributors of methane is the termite, which increases greatly in number where there is a lot of dead wood (there are an estimated 250 million billion termites on Earth!). Another problem caused by forest destruction.
- O_3 – This occurs as sunlight reacts with the exhaust emissions of the combustion of fossil fuels. This may be during industrial processes or from car exhausts.
- In addition to these gases, CFCs (Chlorofluorocarbons) act as greenhouse gases. These do not exist in nature, their only source is when humans produce them as a result of chemical processes.

These human activities produce greenhouse gases, but does this warm the atmosphere? Of course there is dispute – however:

> There is no doubt that the atmospheric concentrations of carbon dioxide, methane, ozone, and nitrous oxide are increasing, and that the concentration of CFCs will continue to increase until the steps that have been taken to restrict its production and use become effective. Nor is there any doubt that these substances intercept long wave radiation and that such interception could lead to a warming of the lower part of the atmosphere.

Michael Allaby, *Living in the Greenhouse: A Global Warning*, p.99

What is clear is that the global temperature trend has shown increase since the industrial revolution in the 19th century – just the point at which many of the human activities referred to above began.

Another feature of possible climate change of equal concern is:

b) The ozone layer

i) The ozone layer – an explanation

> [Joe Farman, a British atmospheric scientist has shown that] between 1975 and 1984, during the southern hemisphere's spring, the [ozone] layer thinned to almost half its former size.
>
> F Pearce, *Turning up the Heat*, p.13

Whereas ozone is poisonous at low levels, in the Earth's stratosphere it is vital. Here it acts as a protective layer. As radiation from the sun meets O_2 in the stratosphere its energy breaks the bonds holding the oxygen atoms together and can create O_3. This process absorbs some of the U-V radiation. The O_3 molecules are very unstable however and eventually revert to O_2 (oxygen). During this series of chemical reactions, the U-V radiation from the sun is 'filtered' so that less of it reaches the Earth's surface. Ozone is therefore in a constant state of creation and destruction in the stratosphere, but this would balance out if left to itself. However, although the chemistry is very complex, the principle is simple. Other chemical molecules exist in the stratosphere which speed up the destruction of the ozone molecules. This reduces the opportunity to absorb the U-V radiation, so more of it reaches Earth. The chemicals which cause this reaction exist naturally in the atmosphere and so the 'thinning' and 'thickening' of the ozone layer is natural. However, environmentalists are concerned that the relative abundance of ozone molecules is being altered by human activity. In particular the release of certain gases into the atmosphere is speeding up ozone depletion at a significant rate. Possible gases which contribute to the depletion of the ozone layer are: nitrous oxide (N_2O) and methane (CH_4). We have already examined how human activity may be increasing the abundance of these gases in the atmosphere. The major possible contributor is the chlorofluorocarbons (CFCs), both CFC_{13} and CF_2C_{12}. These molecules are man-made, and they are particularly effective at destroying ozone molecules.

ii) The ozone layer – possible effects

U-V radiation is harmful to organic matter. There is the obvious human concern about the increased risk of certain types of skin cancer caused by increased levels of U-V radiation. This is a concern but is less worrying perhaps than the fact that U-V radiation has the potential to damage the proteins as well as the DNA of all living things. In this way U-V could act as an agent in genetic mutation. As DNA replicates, mutations caused by the 'cutting' effect of U-V will be passed on to offspring with unpredictable results.

Also, U-V can directly harm sensitive organisms, and therefore cause alterations in the food chain. It is suspected that it is particularly dangerous for algae in the sea. As this is at the bottom of the food chain, it could have much wider implications. U-V can also harm plants when in strong concentrations. This too may have effects for other forms of life further up the food chain. The effects of all this are unpredictable. What seems to be clear is that one of the Earth's mechanisms for regulating the amount of U-V radiation which reaches the surface is becoming unbalanced.

iii) The ozone layer – the human connection

Many of the ozone-depleting chemicals which exist in the atmosphere are perfectly natural in origin; it is the artificially synthesised chemicals which are the problem. The ozone layer naturally varies in strength with the seasons and, as a natural system, the ozone layer keeps itself in equilibrium. The introduction of artificial chemicals upsets that balance. The major issue is the chlorofluorocarbons. Invented in 1930, they are widely used by industry as coolants, propellants and components of certain products. As these CFCs leak, or are expelled in aerosols for example, they make their way to the stratosphere where they destroy ozone. In September 1987, the Montreal Protocol was signed. This was an agreement reached by a number of nations to cut the production of CFCs significantly. You will be aware that these days most aerosol cans are CFC-free. Also, most industrial processes and commercial products which used CFCs have cut their use drastically or replaced them with other chemicals. However, there remain two problems:

- CFCs are very stable and long-lived. Even if there was no CFC-production anywhere in the world from today, the effects of previous CFCs would still be with us.
- The developing nations of the world may find it more difficult to phase out CFCs than the developed world. The issues behind this are complex, and there will be further discussion of these kind of difficulties in Chapter 4. However, particularly in countries like China, it may still take some time before the use of CFCs ends completely.

3 Pollution

Climate change itself may be caused by pollution; however, there are many other human activities which environmentalists might claim are polluting. The difficulty here is in defining pollution. Humans are also a part of nature, and their activities produce by-products. These products then become part of the system, and sometimes they are problematic. It is also difficult to decide when pollution is carried out on purpose or is an unavoidable part of human life. For example, pouring waste chemicals into a river is obviously pollution, but then so, too, is the run-off of agricultural fertilisers into water courses. One might be considered a crime, the other unavoidable – both are harmful. Pollution takes different forms, and depending upon the circumstances has different effects. Problems caused may depend upon a number of factors:

- the amounts and concentrations of the pollutant
- the nature of the pollutant
- the stability of the pollutant with time
- the location of the pollutant. Some natural systems are more sensitive than others.

We will briefly examine some of the major contemporary pollution issues, and the part which humans might play in them.

a) Population

> ... the optimum number of people is not as large as the maximum the Earth can support; or, as it has been more bluntly expressed, 'There is only one pollution ... people'.
>
> JE Lovelock, *Gaia: A New Look at Life on Earth*, p.122

This may strike you as odd; however, the increasing human population presents all kinds of pollution issues. One theme in environmental issues is the balanced state of the Earth. Like any system, it can only sustain so much of any particular activity. As the human population grows, its need for food and energy increases, as well as the amount of waste it produces. It also requires the displacement of other species as humans require more living-space. The requirement to feed an ever-expanding population puts strain on the Earth's ability to regulate its own systems. For example, it is increasingly common to use marginal land – i.e. land which otherwise would be unsuitable for agricultural use – in order to grow crops. This is made possible by the increased application of man-made fertilisers. These can pollute the atmosphere (e.g. N_2O referred to above), and can also get into our waterways – polluting the seas, our freshwater supplies and the other organisms which depend on them for life. This puts a strain on the system.

Also, with technological development comes industrialisation. As societies become more industry-based, their production of potential pollutants increases. That is not to say that pre-industrial societies do not pollute, just that the extent to which they are able to do so is far less than those societies which have industrialised. Also with the development of technology comes the ability to clean up our act – and this has happened – for example, in the case of CFCs. However, the sheer numbers of humans on the planet might mean that the Earth has to find some new regulatory mechanism which can accommodate this imbalance in species.

b) Pollution as by-product

Fortunately, most people do not engage in polluting activities on purpose. Most pollution is caused as the by-product of some process, industrial or agricultural. In general, again the difficulty is in proving that any particular process or activity causes any particular effect. The science and politics are complex.

i) Acid rain

> Some southern German states have lost over 90% of their silver fir … woods covering 2,000 square miles of Germany's coniferous trees are now damaged … 50,000 Canadian lakes are at risk; in Sweden, at least 18,000 lakes are completely acidified – dead. In Norway, 5,000 square miles of lakes are devoid of fish … This plague is as international as it is invisible, seen only by its effects – sparkling clear lochs where no fish swim … forests where no birds sing; wildernesses where animals are poisoned by eating plants, in turn toxified via infiltration of the roots by metals released from the soil by … acid rain.
>
> S Gordon, *Down the Drain*, pp.124–6

Many industrial processes, as well as car exhaust fumes, produce oxides of sulphur and nitrogen. When these chemicals get into the water cycle, they make the water which they come into contact with more acid. This will begin atmospherically, but as the water precipitates it falls as rain making the seas and rivers, as well as the ground, more acid. This can have damaging effects on certain plants and animals because different species cope with increased acidity in different ways. The food chain is complex and damage at one point can lead to unpredictable results at another.

Acid rain may also react with other chemicals in rocks to release metals like cadmium into the soil – this may be even more harmful than the acid rain itself. What is difficult here is, who pays for the clean-up? The effects of acid rain are often felt far from the rain's cause. Some have argued that governments in one country will be unlikely to want to spend money cleaning up an industry which causes most harm in another country. What has to happen, if acid rain is to be dealt with efficiently, is that – like all pollution – countries have to see that it knows no boundaries, and that it is in everyone's interests to clean up after ourselves.

ii) Air pollution

As of January 2000, leaded petrol is no longer on sale in UK filling stations. The lead in this petrol has been linked to brain damage. The air we breathe is invisible, and so too are many of the pollutants which fill it. The most serious pollutants have been examined in the section on global warming. Many pollutants in the air, as well as being potential greenhouse gases or causes of acid rain, can also be directly harmful to life on Earth. This depends upon their concentration, location and accompanying climatic factors. Many industrial and agricultural processes produce air pollution. Particulate air pollution is easy to spot, particularly when it takes the form of fog or sooty deposits. Some pollutants exist in quantities significant enough to require advanced warning. Many blame poor air quality for increases in cases of asthma and other lung problems. Many weather forecasts on TV now include warnings about levels of air pollutants at certain times of the year, for example the concentrations of carbon monoxide, ozone, oxides of sulphur and nitrogen, benzene and 1–3 butadine.

iii) Land and water-cycle pollution

> For although disaster is plainly imminent, industrial nations bordering [the North Sea] still treat it like a tip … over 3.5 million tonnes of industrial waste and 70 million tonnes of dredged waste and sewage sludge pour into it each year … more pollution comes from shipping discharges … and from the incineration at sea of toxic waste …
>
> S Gordon, *Down the Drain*, p.115

Rivers and seas are particularly prone to pollution. Their fluid nature allows pollutants to spread easily. Their ability to clean themselves up is often limited – particularly in the case of closed seas, like the Black Sea, and the North Sea. Marine life in the oceans can be damaged by pollutants entering from land – often via the rivers. One of the most recent concerns has been PCBs. These are chemical additives once used in the production of plastics, lubricants and pesticides. They mimic hormones, and although banned in many countries, they persist in the environment. It is suggested that PCBs might interfere with foetal development in the womb (see *New Scientist* 7/8/99, p.16). Such pollution can be the result of run-off from agriculture, or the spoil from industrial processes. Of course, the seas are used regularly as dumping grounds for our own waste products, including sewage – which may be dumped completely untreated.

> According to an [EC] survey in 1986, Britain had the very worst record [for beaches polluted by sewage] in Europe: a miserable 44% of our beaches came up to scratch … In the words of an old joke, 'It's not so much like swimming round here, it's more like going through the motions!'
>
> F & P Craig, *Britain's Poisoned Water*, pp.81–2

This sewage can contain, as well as organic matter, considerable amounts of man-made chemicals, and other, solid waste.

Some countries deal with their rubbish in landfill sites. These sites can produce toxic run-off which will eventually reach the seas. Other countries still dump their rubbish at sea, and often close to shore lines. Given that most of our rubbish is not biodegradable, this can present serious problems which last for a long time.

The land too is easily polluted. Industrial and agricultural processes leave chemical residue on the land, and the disposal of waste products is not without problems. One example is the disposal of batteries. Many batteries contain mercury – where such batteries are disposed in landfill sites, the mercury may eventually leak and be taken up by the soil. In turn this is taken up by plants and then by the animals which feed on those plants. This may be passed all the way up the food chain, so that the organism at the top (which is often humans) ingests the build up of mercury which began with the battery leakage. Mercury is extremely toxic.

iv) Nuclear pollution
A by-product of the creation of energy using nuclear power is radioactive material which needs to be disposed of. Some of this material is very dangerous for living organisms, and remains active for a very long period. Nuclear waste has to go somewhere. There have been many suggested solutions and most involve the burying of nuclear waste encased in concrete either at sea or deep underground. Debate still rages about this potentially serious form of pollution, fuelled by the argument that nuclear energy is the most 'green', at least when compared with energy production which produces greenhouse gases. As well as the pollution caused by the disposal of nuclear waste, there is also the ever-present danger of pollution caused by accident. Many opponents of nuclear energy argue that the consequences of a nuclear accident are so grave that they cancel out any potential benefits which might have been gained.

c) Accidental pollution

For many, the most serious forms of pollution are those where accidental release of pollutants occur. This often happens in large quantities, very rapidly, and involves dangerous substances. Pollution of this nature is often more likely to raise debate about the way in which human society operates than the gradual release of pollutants indirectly as in the section above. Such accidental events receive intense media coverage, and their effects are closely monitored, whereas indirect pollution largely goes unreported. Some important accidental pollution events are as follows:

- 1953–1960 – 111 villagers suffer brain damage caused by eating mercury-contaminated shellfish in Minimata bay in Japan.
- December 1984 – 2,500 people die as methyl isocyanate gas escapes from an insecticide plant in Bhopal, India.
- 1986 – Chernobyl nuclear reactor accident. Wide release of radioactivity.

● 1989 – Oil tanker Exxon Valdez spills 40,000 tonnes of oil off the coast of Alaska. Vast numbers of animal and marine species affected.

Of course, these examples of pollution were unintentional. Nevertheless they do show that human activities which create potential pollution are often difficult to control. Many argue that the possibility of such accidents is enough to make us think again about the way we create, and accept the risk of creating pollution in order to satisfy our needs otherwise.

As well as all this, there are many examples of pollution caused directly, not as the result of accident, but on purpose. In efforts to cut costs, save time, or ease the workload, there have been many examples of polluting incidents which have had, or could have had, serious implications.

> For example, some scientific research waste, spontaneously flammable in air or water, was sold to a company for disposal by incineration. The price was £1350 +VAT. However, the company subcontracted the waste to a transfer-station operator at a price of £187. The operator then further sub-contracted it to a landfill operator for £75. At three stages removed from the original sale, who was to know that landfill was dangerous? Luckily the local authority was aware of the situation and intercepted the waste before dumping could take place.
>
> F & P Craig, *Britain's Poisoned Water*, p.55

The very existence of humans on Earth produces a certain amount of pollution, and as our technology advances and our population increases, the levels of pollution increase.

One final set of specific environmental issues remains.

4 Use of the Earth's resources

Human society requires energy. With increased industrialisation comes an increased demand. At present, many of the raw materials we use to provide our energy as well as other needs come from sources which are not infinite – they will eventually run out. Also, the resources of Earth are put to many uses by mankind, but these resources don't always come easy. Their harvesting, the production processes they go through and the fact that they are not easily able to recover from over-use, all have their environmental impact. We have dealt with some of the side-effects of the use of the Earth's resources above. What though, of their own sustainability?

a) Energy production

> The deposit account of world energy is being overdrawn, taking us and our environment into the red. We're burning up our current stocks at a horrendous rate. The time has come to put [the balance] in order before the energy bank goes bust.
>
> D Bellamy & B Quayle, *Turning the Tide*, p.85

i) Fossil fuel dependency

Our technological society is currently based on fossil fuels. These provide not only our energy, but the raw materials for a wide range of products. The extent to which these fossil fuels can sustain our current levels of use is a matter of scientific debate, but all are agreed that fossil fuels are limited. Also there will come a point where the energy required to obtain the remaining fossil fuels will be so high that it will not be justified by the returns available. The ecologist David Bellamy suggests that if we continue our use of fossil fuels at the current rate, then our coal, oil and gas reserves will run out by 2636. However, a 2 per cent increase in fossil fuel consumption will mean that our stocks will run out in 124 years, and a 5 per cent increase will see fossil fuels run out in 2047.

> Someday the Oil Age will be viewed as one of humanity's transitional phases between the brute-force and the clean-tech approaches to life. Fossil fuels themselves will be viewed as a sort of IQ test that the past left for the future. Are you smart enough to learn how to use this stuff, and are you smart enough to stop?
>
> G Easterbrook, *A Moment on the Earth*, p.341

The difficulty is predicting the projected energy requirements of the future, and the extent to which we expect to meet these using current technology based on fossil fuels. What is agreed is that energy consumption is unlikely to decrease or even stabilise in the near future. This is partly because of increased demand in the developed world, but also a result of the increasing energy demands which will be realised as the developing world industrialises. There is also the problem that dependence upon fossil fuels is accompanied by a dependence upon the industries which control it. There are powerful vested interests involved – many oil companies have budgets which are far greater than many of the world's smaller countries. The economic power of industries which control fossil fuels is significant and, many environmentalists will argue, so powerful that our dependence upon fossil fuels may be maintained by these companies' actions. Also, fossil fuel dependency, many will suggest, is currently a significant feature of world politics. The Middle East, for example, is an area of political instability, but it is also rich in fossil fuels, giving it a pivotal role in world economics and politics. Changes in our use of fossil fuels could therefore have political as well as economic implications.

Eventually, however, fossil fuels will run out. What is at issue for our purposes is the extent to which society will have prepared for this eventuality, and the environmental impact of what we do to prepare for this.

ii) Alternative energy production – renewable resources

There are many alternatives to fossil fuels. However, again there is scientific disagreement about the extent to which these alternatives are both environmentally sound as well as economically feasible. Energy production which is considered to use 'renewable resources' incorporates:

- wind power – windmills as they turn can generate electricity;
- wave power and hydro-electric systems – the kinetic energy of flowing water assisted by the forces of gravity can turn turbines which create electricity;
- solar power – absorption of solar radiation by panels produces heat and can also produce electricity by the use of photo-electric cells.

All of these methods of energy production however, are not clear-cut issues. The task for their supporters is to ensure that the benefits far outweigh the drawbacks. The alleged benefits are:

- endless supply of energy, which will not run out;
- environmental impact of renewables claimed by many to be much less harmful than the use of fossil fuels;
- removes dependency on fossil fuels and the economic and political instability which this may foster.

The drawbacks however are:

- energy supply variable. For example, solar energy capture will vary with location;
- involves large initial capital outlay which will take time to recover;
- the plant itself may be unsightly and interfere with the aesthetic value of the landscape (e.g. windmills), or alter the balance of an ecosystem (e.g. damming projects).

For many, renewable energy production provides one of the most complex challenges for environmentalism. On the one hand, it would remove the dependency on fossil fuels, and the environmental degradation which may accompany it. But alternatively the schemes themselves may actually be environmentally suspect. The '3 Gorges' damming project in China is a very good example. This will produce 18,000 megawatts of clean, renewable energy, but it will also submerge vast areas of landscape, not to mention displace thousands of people from their homes. Environmentalists here are truly caught on the horns of a dilemma.

iii) The nuclear alternative

> ... nuclear power is the only means we have to provide ourselves with the electricity we need. That being so we should try to understand what it is, how it works, and to distinguish between genuine risks and those we may perceive but that we exaggerate.
>
> M Allaby, *Living in the Greenhouse*, p.181

> Environmentally the nuclear industry ... provides possibly the greatest threat to our planet's well-being and the survival of the human species. Is it right that we should be trading in poisons which can survive up to a quarter of a million years... Is it right that we should consign our children and grandchildren to the risk of future radiation poisoning, to live their lives on the edge of darkness?
>
> D Bellamy & B Quayle, *Turning the Tide*, p.72

The use of nuclear energy raises strong feelings. Many see it as the clean environmental solution to our energy needs, others as an unpredictable poisoned chalice. The main issues are safety, cost and side-effects. In terms of cost, nuclear power is very competitive. Many argue that this economic edge disappears when you add in the unpredictable costs of the future monitoring of waste materials. To add in the cost of wages for those workers who will monitor waste safety – for the next 250,000 years – makes the unit cost of nuclear energy today actually relatively high.

The nuclear industry claims a very good safety record. Opponents, however, claim that this is not good enough, because the effects of even one accident are potentially so grave. Also the detrimental side-effects of nuclear radiation are so serious that many environmentalists have dismissed it as an alternative to fossil fuel dependency. However, the debate goes on, because there is a need to prepare for when those fuels we currently use finally run out.

iv) Energy efficiency

Many have argued that rather than seek new sources of energy we should simply use the energy we have more efficiently. This may be by energy-saving technology, or adaptations to our lifestyle – for example, cycling rather than using the car. In Britain recently, the cost of road tax for smaller-engined cars which use fuel more efficiently has been lowered in comparison to larger engined-cars. The aim is to encourage fuel efficiency. There are many ways in which the use of energy resources could be cut – it is suggested, for example, that most houses in Britain are not built with energy efficiency in mind. For many efficiency is the solution, not the search for ever more sources of energy to be put to thoughtless and often dubious use.

As well as energy however, human use of other raw materials also requires attention.

b) Resource depletion

Human society uses Earth's resources in abundance. Once again, these resources are not without limit, and, environmentalists claim, unless we restrict our use of the products for which such raw materials are required, then soon these raw materials will run out. The use of the Earth's resources, as well as eating into a finite source of materials, may involve all kinds of polluting side-effects. These effects can harm ecosystems as a whole, and therefore of course, humans too. Currently resources which are likely to be used are:

- mineral deposits, including metallic ores, carbons and hydrocarbons.
- organic materials – for example wood products from managed and non-managed forest sites.
- food resources – for example stocks of fish in the oceans.

The environmentalist argument is that in our use of the Earth's resources we should consider two basic issues. The first is the extent to which the resource which we are using is really necessary. This is a complex question, but is important. The second is the extent to which our use of natural resources takes place in a way which is sustainable. In other words, are these resources being obtained in ways which allow their levels to be sustained for future generations? For example, most countries now employ systems of fishing quotas. This means that at any time, fishing boats may only catch certain amounts of fish. Also these boats' nets should be of a certain size so as to allow the escape of younger smaller fish. The idea here is that stocks therefore will be able to replenish themselves for future use. These quotas however, are often difficult to police, and even where they are abused, punishments are often not in proportion to the possible benefits to be gained by breaking the rules.

Again, however, the principle is simple. The Earth has a limited stock of natural resources. Once these are gone they cannot be replaced.

c) Practical responses

There is agreement that there are only three real options open to us in solving anything which is considered to be an environmental problem:

- adaptation – in response to environmental change we adapt our lifestyle to fit the new set of conditions. The problem with this is that change is unpredictable and may be sudden as well as gradual. Such adaptation might require major lifestyle changes which some might not be prepared to make, especially since the benefits predicted might not happen in their own lifetimes.

- using technology – this is scientifically as well as economically problematic. The Earth's systems are also so complex that it would be difficult to predict accurately the outcome of any such action. It might actually worsen the situation.
- prevention – most are agreed that this is the most profitable response. If we can identify the causes of environmental degradation, then we can put plans into action to deal with these causes before they take effect. This is in fact what the world's governments have tended to do. The only difficulty here is that such preventative measures may not be able to be taken equally around the world. Some may also choose not to for a variety of reasons. The problem is that opinions differ so widely about causes and effects that many are unwilling to take preventative action which will 'cost' them in some way, especially when they are unsure that any actual benefits will accrue.

As you have seen, human society is immensely powerful with respect to the environment. Our lifestyle choices have implications for the state of the planet. Though the science and economics is complicated, there is wide agreement that examining our own environmental ethics, and the actions which result from them, is necessary.

5 Ethical responses

What is at issue throughout this section is the potential for human activity to cause harm to the natural world. In Chapter 1 we explored how various ethical traditions respond to the environment generally. Now we will examine the ways in which those same ethical traditions would be likely to respond to the specific issues just outlined.

a) Egoism

i) If climate change results from my actions then that is acceptable provided that such climate change does not ultimately have negative consequences for me. For example, if the egoist could be shown that using aerosols was more likely to lead to an increased risk of skin cancer, he may forego the relatively small benefits of the former for the greater benefits of the latter.

ii) Pollution is a problem where it affects me. The egoist would have to be convinced that any of his activities which were polluting the planet would eventually cause him harm. There might be differences between egoists here, because some might take a longer-term view than others. For example, an egoist with children might believe that it is in his best interests to lessen pollution because it might have consequences for his children after his death (they are, after all his future). A childless egoist may not respond in this way.

iii) Egoism would give little regard to the use of the Earth's resources, unless the egoist took the same view as the one above. Much of the issue surrounding the use of planetary resources relates to sustainability. The fear is not for now, but for the impact that our use now will have on the future of the planet. The egoist might be unconcerned about this. It is beyond his own life-span, therefore it does not really matter.

b) Utilitarianism

i) The utilitarian would have problems with climate change. Clearly if certain actions benefit the majority at the expense of the few, then that is acceptable. However, what is at issue is the extent to which the causes of climate change are worth the effects. A utilitarian might conceivably take the view that the benefits of actions which potentially cause climate change cannot match the drawbacks which they might cause. This is because the utilitarian might feel it necessary to take the longer-term view. For example, let us say that the use of fossil fuels greatly benefits every single human on Earth today. If such use were to cause global warming, then the negative effects of today's pleasures would be felt by generations to come. Such numbers greatly outweigh the present population of the Earth. The utilitarian might therefore reject actions which have potentially global warming results.

ii) Similarly with pollution. The utilitarian would want to be assured that polluting activities benefited the many at the expense of the few, and not the other way around. A utilitarian might therefore be expected to accept a certain amount of pollution for its benefits. However, again if the longer-term view were taken, then the utilitarian would have to think carefully. This would be particularly the case with reference to nuclear power, whose costs and potential drawbacks will long outlast the benefits now. Also if the utilitarian were to count all living species in his thinking, then this too will affect his views. Pollution does not only affect humans but many other species – even when the only real benefits are usually for humans themselves.

iii) In relation to the use of planetary resources the utilitarian would have to be sure that stocks of materials necessary for a 'happy' life would continue throughout the ages. There would be little benefit to future generations if the planet were devoid of energy or other raw materials in the future. Also, the knowledge that our actions now would be likely to cause this 'suffering' in the future could cause us suffering of a kind now – for example, guilt at robbing future generations of the materials they will need to maximise their own pleasure.

c) Altruism

i) The altruist would also have to weigh things up. The causes of global warming might be beneficial for others now, but the effects might not be so pleasurable. An altruist would need to be convinced that either we could adapt to global warming, fix it, or take preventative action, and that none of these would be harmful for others.

ii) Pollution clearly is harmful. It is also not selective about whom it harms The altruist would want to limit his own activities which were likely to produce pollution which could harm other people. Also, if the altruist took into account non-human life, then his actions may be even more guarded.

iii) The altruist would want to ensure that others would not be harmed by the use of natural resources. This would include those who would be harmed by their extraction and use now, and those who might in future be harmed by their disappearance due to our over-use. There could be conflicting issues at stake here. For example, fishing quotas may seriously harm the livelihoods and the whole way of life for fishing communities now. The altruist would have to be convinced that this was a necessary price to pay for the future stability of fish stocks.

d) Situation ethics

i) To take this approach to climate change would require accurate knowledge of cause and effect. Each action would have to be judged on its own merits in relation to its likely benefits and the extent to which it could contribute to climate change. Such an approach would judge each response to climate change in relation to its likely outcome – and of course this is one of the major difficulties. Clearly if it could be demonstrated that a particular action or lifestyle was likely to create major climate changes, then that action would have to be examined. However, in order to modify that action, this person would have to be sure that such a modification would actually produce real benefits.

ii) For the situation ethicist, pollution too would be judged individually. A certain level of pollution could be accepted provided that the benefits resulting were significant enough individually or globally. In many respects we all respond like this in relation to sewage. Everyone accepts that the removal of sewage is necessary from our homes – most of us, however, arguably do not concern ourselves too much with what happens to it thereafter.

iii) Finally such a view would consider the use of planetary resources necessary in some situations and perhaps not in others. There can be no hard and fast rules in relation to this ethical tradition. It is probably true to say that someone who based their actions on this ethical viewpoint would still want to ensure that there were sufficient planetary resources around for a long time to come, and that the use of these resources now was necessary.

e) Legalism

i) The difficulty here is that since no one can accurately claim that they have all the answers about the causes and effects of climate change, legal development has been slow. Most of the laws in relation to this issue are in the form of directives and guidelines, and as yet many actions which are considered likely to cause climate change on an individual basis are outside the scope of the law. Of course there are some laws: cars in the UK must now pass exhaust emission tests as part of the MOT test. The legal approach to issues here is more often at the level of production processes in industry – for example the phasing out of CFCs. However, individuals are encouraged by incentives to take up lifestyles which are 'friendlier' towards the threat of climate change. Governments in many countries, for example, have begun programmes which encourage cycling and the use of public transport as opposed to the use of the private car. The legalist will want to ensure that he is aware of the legal attempts to limit the suspected causes of climate change.

ii) With respect to pollution, the legal situation is much clearer. Many acts of pollution are considered criminal when intentional. Even when pollution is accidental, those who have caused it may still feel the force of the law upon them. For example, when oil spills occur there are usually heavy fines for the companies involved – as well as massive clean-up bills. The legalist is on surer footing with respect to pollution.

iii) The legal situation with respect to the use of resources varies widely. Many resources are strictly regulated – fish quotas have been discussed already. Others, however, are less so, the only legal restrictions being on the side effects of the methods by which such resources are obtained. As yet, there are no clear legal guidelines about the extent to which a country may exploit its natural resources. The exception to this is that the exploitation of resources in certain locations is generally prohibited. For example, in the UK, sites of special scientific interest (SSSIs), other scenic areas and many heritage sites may not be used for the exploitation of resources.

The major problem is that the legal situation varies across the world. Some countries are more likely to exploit resources in areas which are environmentally sensitive. The Brazilian rainforest is the best-known example. This is often because these countries feel that the economic argument in favour of the exploitation of these resources is stronger than the scientific one against. One development in this area is where sites are designated world heritage sites. In this situation, other governments help one country to look after its important sites, by assisting these countries economically. In return these countries preserve rather than exploit such areas.

f) Religious authority

i) Religious approaches differ widely, and some might argue that organised religion has been slow to respond to specific environmental issues until now. Many fundamentalists in Islam, Judaism and Christianity might argue that no response is required. They would suggest that the renewal of nature which we have spoilt is God's task. That this can only be achieved once people have turned to God and put right their relationship with him.

However, many others within these faiths might see this as 'burying your head in the sand'. They would argue that God gave humans the unique ability (and the unique duty) to preserve nature, and therefore they should do so. Christians, for example, have often been instrumental in environmental organisations. Christianity teaches that the Earth belongs to God, and that humans are its stewards. Therefore all Christians have a responsibility to ensure that environmental problems are tackled when they occur. Also, as part of their stewardship role, they should try to stop environmental problems occurring by responsible and sustainable use of the planet. Similarly, Buddhists believe in limiting their own environmental impact where possible. The Buddhist ideal is to take only what is given, and to respect all life. Such an attitude should lead to concern for the environment generally.

ii) Concern for others is important in all religions. The 'Golden Rule' in Christianity is that you should treat others the way you would like to be treated yourself. There is no reason why this should not also apply to the environment generally, particularly as one's actions will lead to consequences for others.

The Hindu concept of non-violence (ahimsa) means that every individual should treat all living things fairly and gently. Actions which could be considered harmful to the environment would go against this spirit of ahimsa. Besides which, for the Hindu, treating other things badly, including nature, would result in bad karma and therefore not help the individual to escape rebirth. In this respect therefore, acts which result in pollution, intentionally or otherwise, would be considered ethically unacceptable.

iii) Religions like Christianity also place much emphasis on using the Earth's resources wisely. In Christianity there is concern that the desire for material wealth does not get in the way of spiritual progress. Should the Earth be seen as nothing other than a source of material wealth which can be plundered at will, then this could lead to an attitude which is materialistic. Such an attitude will get in the way of spiritual development. It may lead to riches on Earth but not in Heaven, as the Christian focuses on material improvement. Christians would also wish to see resources used sustainably so that future generations do not have to suffer for our benefit now. This would be part of the general Christian ethic of concern for others.

Buddhist teaching about taking only what you need would involve rejection of over-consumption and the plundering of the Earth's resources to meet what would be considered greed not need. This would apply globally as a species, as well as individually. A Buddhist might well argue that applying such an ethic will lead to a wise and sustainable use of the Earth's resources.

6 Conclusion

The causes and effects of climate change are still much debated. This is principally the case in relation to the science behind the issue. However, there are also disagreements politically and economically about the relationship between the costs of any changes to human behaviour and the likely benefits. At any rate, these specific issues are very complex.

Pollution, when dramatic and accidental is always condemned. However, when it is gradual, and an accepted side effect of other processes, it may tend to go unnoticed. Again the issue largely revolves around the extent to which any response to it is justified by the likely benefits resulting from such a response.

There are widely different approaches to the use of natural resources. Many take a cautious approach, preferring to ration what we know we have. Others seek alternatives. Yet others may place their 'faith' in the hope that somehow science and technology will come up with the right answers should we run out of anything in the near future. Most perceive the need to balance what we require with what is available, at least until such times as we are able to access viable alternatives. Once again, one of the important issues is the extent to which people and governments are willing to invest now for benefits in the future which are not necessarily guaranteed.

Study guides

Summary List

You should build your study notes on the following:

- What are the possible causes and effects of global warming?
- What are the possible causes and effects of the depletion of the ozone layer?
- What are the possible causes and effects of pollution?
- To what extent are these environmental 'problems' natural events?
- To what extent does human activity contribute to these 'problems'?
- To what extent should the Earth's resources be used by human society, and when does use become over-use?
- To what extent do the ethical traditions studied help in responding to the questions which these environmental issues raise?
- How might environmental 'costs' and 'benefits' be measured in relation to the three specific environmental issues examined?

Examination Guide

Questions in this area are likely to ask you to do the following:

- Demonstrate knowledge of the scientific issues behind each environmental issue.
- Show that you are aware of the complexity of the issue. i.e. that it involves economic, political, social, ethical and behavioural dimensions.
- Show that you can put many of these different aspects 'together' and arrive at reasoned conclusions.
- Be able to apply the various ethical traditions to a particular environmental issue.
- Reach your own conclusions about the causes, effects and possible solutions to the specific environmental issues examined.

Sample Essay Question and Guide

'Pollution is a necessary side-effect of economic growth.' To what extent might a utilitarian agree?

1. You are being asked to take a particular viewpoint so be wary of simply writing your own opinion (unless you happen to consider yourself utilitarian!)
2. Start by briefly defining the terms – what is economic growth, what is pollution, how are the two linked?
3. You may also like to set out your own brief explanation of the utilitarian point of view generally.
4. This essay is effectively asking you to consider:
   - whether or not pollution is a side-effect of economic growth.
   - if it is, to what extent it is unavoidable/necessary.
   - whether or not economic growth is desirable.
   - what 'price' we should be prepared to put on such economic growth in terms of potential environmental harm.
   - how a utilitarian would view these aspects of the question.
5. Remember that utilitarianism seeks the maximisation of happiness for the greatest number. In relation to pollution therefore, any action which might produce benefit (economic growth) must not be outweighed for the greatest number by drawbacks (the effects of pollution). It is up to you in the substance of your essay to show how far this could be the case generally or in relation to any specific examples you have studied.
6. Finally, your conclusion should be from a utilitarian perspective not your own, so the final section of your essay should begin something like this:

So, in conclusion, it would be fair to say that a utilitarian would agree/disagree/both/be unsure that pollution is a necessary side-effect of economic growth because …

Typical Examination Questions

1. 'Global warming reflects human arrogance in relation to nature.' To what extent would you agree?

2. How far is the depletion of the ozone layer an issue for religious people?

3. 'We should only be concerned with pollution for our own sake.' How might a utilitarian respond to this statement?

4. 'Nuclear energy is the most 'green' solution to the future energy crisis.' How far would you agree?

5. 'The environmental benefits of sustainable sources of energy are outweighed by their drawbacks.' To what extent do you agree?

6. 'Egoism offers no hope in the struggle to balance human need with the environmental degradation caused in meeting that need.' How might an egoist respond?

7. 'In trying to balance the need to preserve nature with the need to exploit it, human interests should always come first.' Choose ONE of the ethical traditions you have explored and show how far it might agree or disagree with this statement.

Activities

This section should involve you in a fair amount of background reading so that you are comfortable with the very complex issues under discussion. Remember that there will be numerous conflicting points of view in relation to these issues, not only about causes and effects, but about what should/should not be done about them. You should keep a scrapbook for this part of the course, there are regular comments about these issues in magazines and newspapers, and you should aim to have your information as up to date as possible. In particular, you may find it helpful to turn much of the information you get hold of into diagrammatic form. For example, with respect to global warming you might draw up a diagram as follows using a mixture of words and illustrations:

Suggestions for Further Reading

1 *Britain's Poisoned Water*: F&P Craig; Penguin, 1989, ISBN 0 14 011050 X

2. *Down the Drain*: S Gordon; Optima, 1989, ISBN 0 356 17944 3

3. *Turning up the Heat*: F Pearce; Paladin, 1989, ISBN 0 586 08915 2

4. *Living in the Greenhouse*: A Global Warning: M Allaby; Thorsons, 1990, ISBN 0 7225 2258 4

5. *Global Environmental Issues*: PM Smith & K Warr (Eds) Hodder & Stoughton, 1991, ISBN 0 340 53362 5

6. *Ecology Facts*: M Allaby; Hamlyn,1986, ISBN 0 600 39723 0

3 The Treatment and Rights of Animals

1 Introduction

KEY ISSUES
- What rights do animals have?
- How are those rights to be decided?
- What are the responsibilities of a dominant species?
- Is the relationship between humans and animals open to ethical debate or just a natural relationship outside the scope of ethics?
- How are animals treated by the human species and what are the potential implications of this for life on Earth now and in the future?
- How do various ethical theories respond to animal issues?

The test of a society is how it treats its animals

M K Gandhi

'The rights of animals' is rarely out of the news. Whether it is hunting, experimentation, the use of animals for food or simply a philosophical debate about what rights animals should have, the topic is difficult to avoid.

Earth supports an incredible diversity of life. It would seem that every possible opportunity for existence has been grasped by life on Earth. Darwinian evolutionary theory suggests that all living things on Earth presently exist due to their ability to adapt to an ever-changing environment. This change can be gradual, as in the case of climate change or sudden as in the consequences of meteor strikes.

It is reasonable to state that the most successful species now living on Earth is the human species. Although many other life forms have advantages over humans in particular respects, overall humanity has the upper hand. This power of humans may have effects not only on the regulatory systems of the planet, as you have seen, but also on the other organisms with which we share Earth. There may never have been such a successful creature as man. However though this success confers much that we consider as rights, it may also involve a considerable degree of responsibility.

There are many points of connection between humans and animals. This section explores the central ethical questions which this interface raises.

2 The moral status of animals

The question of whether or not animals should or can have rights is one of the central questions in this area of environmental ethics.

a) Animals should have no rights

It might be argued that since animals are not human they do not require to be given rights. Rights are only appropriate for beings which have self-awareness, have some sort of social system, can express their desires and can be held accountable for their actions. Some will argue that rights can only be attributed in the context of a contract where all parties involved understand the requirements of the contract agreement.

Rights imply responsibilities – you cannot have rights unless you are prepared to accept the limitations on your actions which those rights confer. For example, humans have the right not to be killed. In accepting the benefits of this we also accept the responsibility of not killing others. Animals cannot do this. In the same way that it makes no sense to charge a lion with murder for killing its prey, it makes no sense to criticise a human for inflicting pain on an animal.

However, philosophers like Peter Singer respond to this by claiming that if we accept this then we accept too that seriously mentally handicapped humans have no more rights than animals. There are many humans who have no more self-awareness than animals, and cannot accept the 'contract' of social rules. Just as no one would be likely to accept that such humans should have no rights, we should not think therefore that animals should have no rights either. We accept that a human has certain rights because it is a human, therefore we must accept that animals should have rights because they are animals. In other words, there is no reasonable ethical foundation for withholding all rights from animals. In this argument, an animal has intrinsic, or inherent value – its value comes from itself not from what we think it can or cannot do.

> When it comes to the case for animal rights, then, what we need to know is whether the animals that, in our culture, are routinely eaten, hunted, and used in our laboratories, for example, are like us in being subjects of a life. And we do know this. We do know that many ... of these animals are the subjects of a life ... and so have inherent value if we do. And since, in order to arrive at the best theory of our duties to one another, we must recognize our equal inherent value as individuals, reason – not sentiment, not emotion – reason compels us to recognize the equal inherent value of these animals and, with this, their equal right to be treated with respect.
>
> Tom Regan, *In Defence of Animals*, p.16

Others would argue that the relationship between humans and animals is not an ethical one, but simply a biological one. Humans are designed to kill to eat. This is no more an ethical question than whether or not it is right to sleep. Using animals for human benefit is simply a fact of our biological existence – to even consider the ethics of this is pointless.

b) Animals should have some rights

Some have developed the idea of intrinsic value and tried to argue that because animals share certain fundamental human characteristics, this points to their value as living beings. It is argued that because animals can feel pain and suffer much as we do, they should automatically be protected from such suffering at our hands. For example, in New Zealand there was recently an attempt to confer almost human rights on chimpanzees, because they share 99 per cent of their DNA with humans. This is taken to mean that they are 'almost human'. If this is the case then surely they should have some rights. Others respond to this by arguing that certain worms share 75 per cent of human DNA, but no one would suggest that this makes them three-quarters human. The value of an animal over, say, a plant is that an animal is clearly more like a human than a plant is and should therefore be more entitled to rights than any other form of life (see *New Scientist*, 15/5/99 pp.26–30).

Christians like Andrew Linzey argue that animals should have some rights because of their status as creatures of God. Their value also comes from their position of vulnerability. Linzey also argues that one fundamental Christian principle is the duty of the strong to help the weak. He suggests that we can assume animals to be 'weak', and because of this they demand our protection.

> I argue … that we need to go even further: that a morally satisfying interpretation of our obligations to animals cannot simply rest with a claim for equal consideration as advanced by some animal liberationists. Drawing upon the notion of divine generosity exemplified in the person of Jesus, I suggest that the weak and defenceless should be given not equal, but greater, consideration. The weak should have moral priority.
>
> Andrew Linzey, *Animal Theology*, p.28

Other philosophers have taken a similar stand by arguing that the status of humans as the most powerful species on the planet implies a special responsibility. We have evolved to the point where we can be considered nature's caretakers. To this extent we have a responsibility to animals.

Yet another argument is that animals should have some rights because how they are treated has direct implications for humanity, and its own moral well-being. Put simply, if we can accept cruelty to animals, then we are one step closer to being able to accept cruelty to humans. According to this argument, therefore, giving animals rights acts as a kind of moral buffer on human behaviour.

c) Animals should have the same rights as humans

Many animal activists uphold this argument, on the basis that animals are not morally or practically any different to humans. Their argument would be that living things have an intrinsic value which is not dependent upon any outside factor. All living things deserve to be protected from cruelty which is unnecessary. Opponents of this might suggest that the difficulty here is where to draw the moral line before the whole idea becomes meaningless.

> Giving farm animals more space, more natural environments, more companions does not right the fundamental wrong, any more than giving lab animals more anaesthesia or bigger, cleaner cages … Nothing less than the total dissolution of commercial animal agriculture will do this, just as, for similar reasons … morality requires nothing less than the total elimination of hunting and trapping for commercial and sporting ends. The rights view's implications, then as I have said, are clear and uncompromising.
>
> Tom Regan, *In Defence of Animals*, p.25

What do we mean by 'the same as humans'? Even the strictest vegan animal rights activist accepts that the taking of some forms of life is necessary for his survival. What if it were to be conclusively demonstrated that plants can feel pain, suffer and 'fear' for their own lives in the same way that animals and humans can? To exist, one necessarily requires to depend on other life-forms for survival. Once we start attributing human rights to all living things, then we are on a slippery slope to being unable to lead a normal human life at all.

Others will suggest, however, that the issue of rights centres on the causing of unnecessary harm. For example, it would not be wrong to kill an animal which was attacking you and threatening your life. However, most harm caused by humans is avoidable, and it is this avoidable suffering which the application of full human rights would help to avoid.

3 Specific themes

Ethical questions often arise in situations of conflict where one person, group or society's needs – or usually more specifically wants – are different from another's. Issues related to the treatment of animals are no different. The most relevant issues for our purposes in this book are probably:

- cruelty towards animals
- the exploitation of animals
- the status of animals.

Each of these elements is interconnected – a common feature of ethical discussion. Animals and humans are part of a living system which inevitably involves some degree of compromise and accommodation. In natural systems it is arguable that this reaches a natural state of equilibrium. However, in a world where humanity is dominant, this balance might be upset – at least this is a very current environmentalist's view. It is that very lack of balance which might actually lead to some of the dilemmas which will follow.

a) Cruelty towards animals

The problem here is in identifying exactly what counts as cruelty. Clearly when animals are directly mistreated, as in the case of neglected animals brought to light by organisations such as the RSPCA, that can be said to be cruelty. It is fairly obvious that when an animal has been starved or beaten, this is cruel. However, many animal activists might argue that the treatment of animals in the slaughterhouse is equally cruel, but that because it is 'sanitised' by being hidden away and surrounded in a certain amount of secrecy, this cruelty is tolerated by the vast majority. Similarly, animal rights' supporters might suggest that how animals are routinely treated in experimental laboratories is most certainly cruel, but that this produces a different response from society because of the perceived value of the work being done. The Research Defence Society, which supports the use of animals in experiments, highlights this 'confusion' by comparing the statistics:

> In the average lifetime we will eat 100 chickens, ten pigs, two cows. At the same time, two animals will be used in experiments on our behalf.
>
> Research Defence Society

Put simply, what makes something cruel is a matter of opinion. When cruelty is dramatic it will always make the headlines, but when it is more subtle, or depends upon someone's point of view, then it is more difficult to identify and challenge.

Furthermore, there is the difficulty of the justification of cruelty. Most right-thinking people (in the study of ethics, that is in itself a troublesome concept) believe that purposeless cruelty is wrong. However, it is probably true that most will accept some degree of direct or indirect cruelty if it can be shown that there might be some greater gain to be had from this. For example, the use of animals in experiments may be cruel, but if it produces helpful scientific progress then perhaps it is morally justifiable. Once more this depends on your point of view – in what circumstances might an act which could be considered cruel also be considered justifiable? (For the results of a Mori Poll on these issues, see *New Scientist*, 22/5/99, pp.26–31.)

b) The exploitation of animals

A similar problem concerns us here – what exactly is exploitation? For a human this can seem obvious. It might be where someone is not paid 'a fair day's pay for a fair day's work'. Humans can also express directly or otherwise their dissatisfaction with the way in which they are treated. Not so with animals. Also, to decide whether an animal is exploited or not is more difficult, and may depend upon objective assessment by someone with a great deal of experience of a particular species, or even particular animals within that species – for perhaps what is acceptable to one performing tiger is unacceptable to another. Exploitation might mean:

- where an animal is made to behave in a degrading way
- where an animal is made to behave in an unnatural way
- where an animal is overworked
- where an animal is not appropriately rewarded for its efforts

All of these possible modes of exploitation can be the subject of debate and disagreement, and that is part of the ethical problem. For example, many support the use of animals in circuses by arguing that the activities undertaken by the animals are simply extensions of what they would do in the wild. Others may accept this to a limited extent, but argue that the animal's actions go beyond reflecting wild behaviours and become degrading, as one animal activist put it:

> elephants may indeed stand on their hind legs in the wild, but they will do so when they choose, not wearing a ballerina's tutu nor at the bidding of a fat man in a top hat.

Since humans first appeared on Earth there has been some form of symbiotic relationship between mankind and certain other species. Each gave something and each received something in return – the human/dog relationship being the most obvious example. The problem is when that relationship becomes weighted in favour of one species over another. In the same way that it is often difficult for us to work out when someone is laughing with us or laughing at us, perhaps the difference between use and exploitation is difficult to pinpoint – especially when the creature which might be being exploited has limited powers of communication with us (or should that be the other way round?).

c) The status of animals

The previous two practical concerns lead us to this more abstract one. Many people argue that every living thing has an intrinsic value which should not be questioned by any outside agent. Much of the argument centres on the belief that animals should be treated in a way which does not take into account their usefulness for us. As far as humans are concerned most agree that there are some 'inalienable rights', i.e. rights which we should all have just because we are human and for no other reason. Similarly, many would suggest that animals should be valued for what they are, and that they should be treated accordingly. However, are there limits to equality? One critic of the animal rights movement states:

> animals rights, animal rights … the logical end of all this talk about animal rights is that they should presumably be given the vote.

Clever though this is it misses the point. It also highlights a considerable danger when talking about animal rights, that of attributing anthropomorphisms to animals (assuming that they will like/dislike things in a 'human' way). The point is not, so a supporter might argue, that animals should be accorded certain inalienable rights because they should be treated equally with humans, but because they are animals. The value of a monkey, so to speak, should and could only ever be measured in monkey terms. The real desire is to allow animals their own rights, not burden them with those which may only be appropriate to us.

This issue gives rise to one of the most thorny areas of ethical debate in the whole human/animals area. If animals were to be given the same moral, social, political, scientific, theological and philosophical (to name but a few) status as humans, what would be the implications for the connection between animal and human life? For example if the concept of 'murder' were to be extended to animals, then we would all have to switch to vegetarianism overnight or risk prosecution.

4 General viewpoints

Before considering some of the actual issues surrounding the treatment of animals, we must explore briefly some more general points of view.

a) Pessimism

Firstly, there are those who think that the present treatment of animals is wholly negative. Such people will point out that instances of direct animal cruelty have increased considerably during the recent past – this is an obvious example. However, they will also point to what they will label as our seemingly increasing indifference to the plight of animals. For example, it might be claimed that farming practices have become so developed that they now mean that animals are treated as nothing more than commodities. When technology was introduced to the rearing of animals, what was humane became irrelevant. Factory farming is the most prominent example of this. Also, the rate at which animal species are becoming endangered and extinct seems to many to be spiralling out of control. The use of animals for their furs and other body parts shows no sign of slowing down – in fact some have argued that world political upheaval (such as the end of the USSR, for example) has provided ready markets and mechanisms for the distribution of the exotic and the endangered. It may also be pointed out that as humanity increasingly exploits the land, the animal species which depend upon it for their very existence are also victims. In short, the treatment of animals by humans is a cause for pessimism.

> Britain has a reputation as a nation of animal lovers, but our treatment of the animal creation is frequently bad and occasionally scandalous. In vivisection laboratories, factory farms and slaughterhouses, animals are treated as mere machinery. This cruelty continues because they are valued only in terms of their usefulness to humans instead of their worth in themselves.
>
> Tim Cooper, *Green Christianity*, p.246

b) Optimism

Alternatively there may be a more optimistic response. Although it might be conceded that the treatment of animals requires thoughtful improvement, there are many who believe that we are at least heading in the right direction. For example, who would have imagined meat-free meat substitutes twenty years ago? Some might argue that far from being thoughtlessly cruel, there are advantages for the animals of certain factory farming practices, and as farmers learn from their mistakes things will improve. An increasing environmental awareness, coupled with increasing technological ability may actually improve the treatment of animals considerably. Many of the early, perhaps misguided, enthusiasms for factory farming, for example, have been scaled down as the public rejected the resulting produce. Farmers have responded to a developing sympathetic awareness on the part of consumers by adapting their practices in accordance with guidelines suggested by organisations like the RSPCA – for example the 'freedom foods' range. As far as animal experimentation is concerned, it was recently announced that the last two UK licences for cosmetic testing on animals were voluntarily given up by the companies who held them. Some would argue that as humanity better understands its own place in the universe it is learning to respond sensitively to the needs of other species too, and that this better understanding will itself lead to improvements in practice. An example of this is the proposed 'resurrection' of the quagga. This animal, closely related to the zebra died out at the turn of the century. A scientist has isolated quagga DNA in zebras and is now selectively breeding zebras which exhibit quagga-like traits. He hopes that within the next 50 years or so we will see the return of the quagga – an animal hunted to extinction by humans. This is a clear example of where we can identify mistakes in the past and then put them right.

c) Realism

Finally there is a trend of thinking which we might term realism (or what Greg Easterbrook calls eco-realism).

274 Extinctions per Day, or Maybe One a Year

Roughly since the 1970s, ecologists have claimed a rising degree of species loss caused by human activity. And in this same period researchers have supposed the natural world to contain far more species than once believed. These two trains of thought are barrelling toward each other on the same track.

Greg Easterbrook, *A Moment on the Earth*, p.556–7

This takes the view that the relationship between mankind and the animals is always going to be complex and that tinkering with it won't change the natural predator/prey relationship which animals and humans are always going to have. For this way of thinking, life is a struggle which the fittest will survive. In the same way that a lion selects the weakest of the herd for death, human activity naturally similarly 'selects' the weakest species which then either evolve mechanisms for survival or die out. For example, such an eco-realist might consider the slaughter of animals for food as aesthetically unpleasing and a little clinical, but perfectly natural nevertheless. The logical outcome of this view might be that little time should be spent agonising over the fate of animals, because neither we nor they are capable of transcending our natural impulses anyway. This would lead to the conclusion that humans and animals will find a point of balance somewhere along the line, and that cannot be hurried by any form of supportive action on behalf of the animal world. An eco-realist might state that we should not underestimate nature's ability to withstand whatever we (relatively puny) humans throw at it – and this includes any of our potential assaults on the animal kingdom. Perhaps nature finds a way to get the balance right. Some have argued that the BSE crisis is of this kind. It is essentially a biofeedback loop which responds to maltreatment of one species by another. Put simply, if you feed cows the brain and spinal cords of sheep, then perhaps you should not be too surprised if this results in a development which harms those carrying out the activity, i.e. BSE caused by humans causing CJD which kills humans.

5 The issues

Before considering the wider ethical and philosophical debates more generally, you should briefly explore some of the most often discussed animal concerns. As you work through this section you should consider:

- What are the arguments used to support/reject particular points of view?
- What concrete evidence is used to strengthen these points of view?
- How do you evaluate the worth of the various arguments?

a) Farming practice

The discussion here centres both on the extent to which animals are treated fairly while being farmed, and how they are slaughtered. Opponents might argue that all animal farming is intrinsically cruel, because the idea of raising something just so that you can profit from its death is morally objectionable. They might also focus on particular farming practices, especially factory farming. This is where animals are kept in controlled conditions, usually in a man-made environment. There are certainly instances of abuse in this system; for example, the farrowing crate where sows are tethered in concrete pens where they are unable to move, functioning simply as milk producers for their offspring. The notorious veal crates, now outlawed in the UK but still in use in other EU countries, are another emotive and widely regarded example of the negative aspects of animal farming. These, along with battery hens have probably strengthened the case of the anti-farming lobby considerably.

> The factory farm is one of the more inappropriate technologies of this century: It requires high inputs of capital and energy to carry out a simple, natural process ... the animal factory pulls our society one long, dark step backward from the desirable goal of a sane, ethical relationship with other beings and the natural world.
>
> Jim Mason, *In Defence of Animals*, p.89–90

In addition to this direct cruelty, there is also the question of cruelty which is more indirect. For example, milking cows are routinely made pregnant year after year (often artificially). This encourages their milk production and increases yield. Soon after giving birth their calves are taken from them. It could be argued that this is indirectly a cruel practice – as is the habit of slaughtering these same cows at the end of their productive life. Even fervent vegetarians often overlook the fact that the production of milk may have some ethically undesirable side-effects.

> Farmers make certain efforts not to get to know their animals too well as individuals ... At this level of detachment, the animals, like motor cars or packets of crisps, can be abstracted to the status of mere units of production.
>
> Research by James Serpell in, *The Status of Animals*, p.164

Other forms of inappropriate treatment might be the use of artificial hormones administered to maximise meat ratios. There have been a number of recorded incidents where the use of such hormones has led to some rather unpleasant side-effects for the animals concerned. Many feel that this tampering with 'nature' is unacceptable, though it is probably fair to say that any domestication of animals for consumption has involved some 'unnatural' intervention by humanity. The issues surrounding genetic manipulation are similar, though again farmers might argue that such manipulation of breeding stock has taken place since farming began.

Responses to these concerns generally take the following form:

● Farming is a natural function. It may not be aesthetically pleasing but is necessary.
● Any malpractice in farming can be adequately dealt with by the very strict legislation which presently surrounds the industry. The legal constraints on modern farmers ensure that livestock is better treated, and the product much safer than it has ever been.

- Farming practice is led by economic necessity. Any practices which people find ethically objectionable only take place because the alternatives are too expensive, and because the consumer is unwilling to shoulder the burden. In other words, farmers cannot be blamed for trying to make a living. Everyone has a part to play in being prepared to pay the cost of ethically-produced meat.
- The modern farm is far superior to the kind of idyllic fantasy many people have about farming in the past. As are modern slaughter methods which are governed by strict regulations resulting in more humane killing than in the days when the slaughtering would have been crudely done at the farm itself.
- All farming practice cannot be damned for the malpractice of a few high-profile cases.
- Farming, by definition, involves interfering in the life-cycle and lifestyles of farm animals. Further intervention, like the use of artificial hormones is just an extension of this intervention.

The basic issues involved in farming are:

- What right does one species have to cultivate another species for food?
- How should animals be treated when being reared for meat and subsequently slaughtered?
- To what extent should farming utilise 'unnatural' techniques when rearing animals?
- What counts as an 'unnatural' practice?

b) Hunting

There are at least three categories of hunting:

- Hunting for food
- Hunting as sport
- Hunting as a means of population control.

i) Arguments in favour of hunting for food

- People need to eat. This is particularly true of indigenous populations where hunting is a traditional way of life and provides all dietary requirements or supplements them to some extent.
- It is a natural process – and has the incidental benefit of maintaining the balance of species.
- There are often no alternatives.
- Traditional hunters are skilled in ensuring that the animal does not suffer unnecessarily.

  many [hunters] express considerable admiration and affection for the animals they kill, viewing the quarry not as a victim, but rather as a worthy opponent in a strange game of life and death. Perhaps more surprisingly, none that I spoke to derived any pleasure from the actual business of killing; claiming instead that the social dimension, and the opportunity to express one's skill as a marksman, were by far the most important attractions of their sport.

James Serpell, *The Status of Animals*, p.163

ii) Arguments against hunting for food

- It is no longer necessary. If people require to eat meat then this can be provided in much more humane ways.
- Traditional peoples often abandon many of their traditional practices in favour of alternatives made possible by modern technology. Why should they continue hunting?
- Hunting has been shown to cause the hunted animal severe distress (though there have been some recent scientific challenges to this).
- Hunting has wider environmental implications. Hunting of one species can inadvertently harm another, as one element of the food chain is put out of balance affecting entire ecosystems.
- Modern hunting practices may lead to the death of other species. An example of this is where drift-nets (termed 'walls of death' by Greenpeace) have killed dolphins accidentally while being used to catch tuna.
- There is a difference between the hunting of animals for food where the amount taken is just enough to support life and where it is merely another example of the human tendency towards over-consumption.

The environmental movement has often found itself caught in a dilemma here because it is usually keen to uphold the rights of indigenous peoples against the encroachment of technology. However, this might also mean inadvertently supporting the killing of endangered species. For example, native Canadians are allowed by the International Whaling Commission to hunt a set number of whales each year for food and to maintain traditional practices. Some native Canadians themselves have campaigned against this claiming that it is no longer necessary.

The more difficult issue, particularly in the UK recently has been the issue of hunting for sport.

iii) Arguments in favour of hunting for sport

- It ensures that traditional country practices are maintained.
- It has the beneficial side effect of keeping troublesome species' populations down and so protecting farm livestock and crops.
- The number of animals hunted for sport is very small.
- Skilled hunters with well-trained dog-packs can ensure that the kill is quick and humane.

iv) Arguments against hunting for sport

- It is not necessary. If the numbers of animals hunted are so small, then they surely cannot do too much damage to the farming industry.
- 'Traditional practices' depend on your point of view. If something is wrong, its continuation cannot be justified on the basis of upholding tradition alone.
- Organised hunts actually do more damage to the countryside than do the animals hunted.
- 'The kill' is rarely quick and humane.

This issue has generated a great deal of debate in the UK and is often complicated by divisions based on social class and town/country. It is arguable that 'the traditional hunt' has been portrayed as simply an excess of the wealthy. Often hunt-saboteurs have been portrayed as 'lower class' and/or 'townies' lacking in any real understanding in countryside matters. Both of these extremes are probably largely stereotypes, but as far as the discussion about the issues in the media is concerned, this has probably gone some way to defining the debate. As an ethical issue it is often difficult to separate the social disagreements from the environmental ones.

Population control or culling also may involve controversy:

v) Arguments in favour of culling

- Certain species compete with humans for food – or have the potential to damage livestock (for example the recent proposed badger cull to halt the spread of bovine TB). In order to avoid potential conflict with humans it is more desirable to selectively cull. This preserves people's livelihoods, and actually ensures that animals are left undisturbed.
- Culling ensures that weaker species are not overrun by stronger ones. Occasionally nature needs a helping hand.
- Culling puts balance back into the system. This might be because a non-native species is killing off a native one (for example red/grey squirrel competition in the UK), or where a species for one reason or another has no natural checks on its population expansion.

vi) Arguments against

- It is rarely wise to interfere with natural systems. They tend to find their own balance without human intervention.
- Culling too often is carried out for economic reasons not scientific ones – and is therefore a misuse of human power.

Culling issues have often been clouded by what some commentators have referred to as the 'cute factor'. For example, the culling of rats rarely produces protest, whereas the culling of baby seals produces quite strong reactions. It can also be culturally determined; for example deer may have bambi-like associations for some, but not in the Scottish Highlands where they are generally regarded as a pest when uncontrolled. It also depends on your understanding of what is native. Recently there has been some attempt to cull rabbits – this has been strongly opposed. But are rabbits native to the UK?

c) Animals as food

Both of these issues indirectly raise the more general question of the eating of meat, and how far one has to go to avoid it if it is considered to be ethically unsound.

i) Arguments in favour of meat-eating

- Humans are naturally carnivorous – we have evolved (or were designed) to eat meat.
- Meat provides energy in concentrations that vegetables can't – it is highly nutritious. The nutritional value of meat makes it a valuable weapon in the fight against hunger and malnutrition.
- The production of meat can be achieved by using vegetable material not fit for humans.
- In some cultures of the world eating meat is necessary, because crop yields are particularly low.
- Meat-eating causes no harm to animals as they are slaughtered humanely, according to very strict laws.

ii) Arguments against meat-eating

- It is unnecessary since all human nutritional requirements can be obtained from non-meat sources.
- It is wasteful – the production of meat requires a disproportionate amount of non-meat produce.
- It is dangerous – meat products are often notoriously unsafe for human consumption.
- It is cruel – the treatment of animals before and during slaughter can never be morally justified.
- Just because we can and have traditionally eaten meat does not mean that we still should.

Even if an individual decides not to eat meat, he may still face problems because there are a variety of options – each with qualifications.

- Avoiding red meat: many eat chicken and fish but avoid beef, pork and lamb. The problem here is that this does not really avoid the issues of potential cruelty and the rights and wrongs of eating other living things.
- Vegetarianism: avoiding all animal produce other than by-products like dairy produce and eggs. This may still leave one with the difficulty of ethical problems associated with dairy produce or egg-production. It seems odd for example, if someone rejects eating chicken but can accept eating chicken foetuses.

● Veganism: all animal produce is avoided. However today even vegans might face the difficulty of 'hidden' animal ingredients in many products – in wine and beer for example. Even more significantly, recently genetic engineering might mean that vegetables may contain animal DNA. Does this change the vegetable's moral status to that of an animal?

Clearly the issues are complex no matter how far one rejects or accepts the use of animals for food.

> The animal liberation ethic demands a basic shift in moral consciousness, a repudiation of human superiority over other species through force. Our way of viewing the world becomes more compassionate, more respectful of the needs of other living beings. The vegetarian lifestyle is both a fundamental and a personal means of affirming such a shift. Confronting the oppression of food animals through vegetarianism lies at the heart of the animal liberation ethic and offers the greatest potential for the radical transformation of society.
>
> Harriet Schleifer, *In Defence of Animals*, p.67

d) The use of animals for cosmetic testing

i) Arguments in favour

● Cosmetic companies have a responsibility for consumer safety. The use of animals provides evidence of the safety of cosmetic products.
● Legislation covering such testing is very strict, and animals do not suffer, nor are they mistreated.
● The use of animals provides the most reliable evidence, and in some cases is the only way to gather such evidence – alternative methods can be unreliable and/or dangerous for humans.
● Cosmetic companies should not be expected to make moral judgments for society. People want cosmetics and they want them to be safe. This requires animal testing.

ii) Arguments against

● It is wrong for one species to use another in this way. Animals do not use cosmetics so they should not be used to test them.
● Despite strict legislation, abuses can occur.
● The evidence is not always entirely reliable. Animals may respond to substances in different ways to humans.
● There are many perfectly satisfactory alternatives. For example, computer modelling, artificial cultures, human testing. Many cosmetic companies survive perfectly well without using animals as test subjects.
● Many tests are repeated unnecessarily.

It may be true that the wind has rather left the sails of this particular issue in the UK. There is now a thriving mainstream cosmetic industry which does not use animals in testing. It would seem that consumer pressure on this issue has led other companies to seek out non-animal testing practices. However, opponents of cosmetic testing point out that animals are still routinely used in non-UK countries, and that even companies who have embraced 'cruelty-free cosmetics' may still use animal products in manufacture.

e) The use of animals in medical testing

Animals are still routinely used by the pharmaceuticals industry to test new drugs and also by 'pure science' while researching disease.

> [scientists] will justifiably claim that they are only doing what the customer demands; and that most of their work will eventually benefit humanity or other animals.
>
> James Serpell, *The Status of Animals*, p.164

i) Arguments in favour

These would reflect exactly the arguments in favour of cosmetic testing with these additions:

- If disease can be cured through the use of animals in testing, then who has the right to deny these benefits to the sufferers?
- Drugs are not cosmetics. It is quite possible to reject cosmetic testing while accepting medical. It is a difference of degree. Ensuring that drugs are safe and effective is considerably more important than ensuring that cosmetics are.
- Even if it were undesirable to use animals, it is often unavoidable. Ethically it would be impossible to use humans for some experiments. For example, one could not give someone cancer in order to test whether a particular drug worked against it or not.
- Medical experiments on animals can benefit animals too. Drugs for animal diseases can be tested.
- The benefits greatly outweigh the sacrifices.

> Faced with human death and suffering, the question of prior relationships is arguably the decisive factor. We regard the death of a human as far worse than the death of an animal, because humans mean so much more to us ... It is not a question of our relative versus our pet, but versus a remote batch of experimental animals that we will probably never know anything about. To disallow the prospect of any therapies for serious diseases that would have depended on such models would be a hard thing indeed ... This is especially so, given that in the home we regard mice as vermin and are prepared to poison or trap them on the grounds of the risk to health.
>
> Wilmut, I, D & A Bruce (Eds), *Engineering Genesis*, p. 155

ii) Arguments against

Similarly these are the same as for cosmetic testing with the following additions:

- If animals are biologically close enough to humans to make the results worthwhile then do we have the right to perform such acts – and if animals are not biologically close enough to humans, what is the value of the experiment?
- Alternative techniques to the use of animals are possible, but because of costs are often ignored.
- A drug for human illness or disease can only effectively be tested on humans. There have been many examples of drugs which have worked on animals but have then failed at the human stage

Perhaps in this issue, more than any other of the animals issues, the portrayal of the 'defenceless creatures v cruel and powerful mankind' has been prominent. Some philosophers, for example Peter Singer, have even talked about humans being guilty of 'speciesism'. It is difficult to strip away emotional responses to this issue – and it is of course debatable whether or not that is always desirable – but there are clearly instances of 'abuses' from both sides of the debate. For example, instances of abuse of animals used in experiments have been well-documented. However it is also true that those who have been involved in 'animal liberation' from laboratories have often acted without thinking through the consequences of their actions. The release of non-native species can have devastating effects on local wild populations.

However, there are many who might argue that even though the issues so far have negative aspects, generally speaking they can be justified through the argument that the human species has its first duty to its own kind – so the use of animals in a way which supports human existence, however undesirable is acceptable.

This is not however, always so easy to justify in the following situation:

f) Performing animals

By 'performing' we mean the practice of having animals display certain actions according to commands. This might mean acrobatic displays by seals in a marine theme park or more problematically the use of animals in circus acts. The arguments here refer to the use of animals as entertainment, though even this classification invites discussion, because it is often difficult to separate what is simply gratuitous entertainment at the animals' expense and what is entertainment justified by its educational value. One might also like to question the idea that animals may be used as educational 'tools' for humans anyway.

i) Arguments in favour

- Performing animals are a great tradition worthy of maintaining and many people depend upon them for their livelihood.
- The animals are well-treated by their trainers.
- The things they are trained to do merely reflect behaviour in the wild.
- Performing animals educate people – this makes people more likely to wish to look after them in the wild.

ii) Arguments against

- Tradition is not a valid reason for continuing such degrading practice.
- There are many instances of cruelty towards performing animals.
- Performing animals often are trained to do quite unnatural things, and these can lead to a lessening of respect for the animal itself.
- This in turn leads to disrespect or indifference on the part of the public. Most people actually learn little from performing animals and so their seeing them will have no effect on the extent to which they support actions designed to help out wild animal populations.

As in other issues, the difficulty here is one of degree. The trouble being that when talking about this as a generic issue we have to engage in dissimilar comparisons. For example, the 'penguin parade' at Edinburgh zoo is one example of 'performing' but it is surely more respectfully handled and educationally valuable than the use of dancing elephants in a circus.

g) Animals as pets

For many, the question of whether or not animals should be kept as pets is hardly in the same league as the issue of performing animals – even though pets are often trained to display certain behaviours which are then labelled as 'tricks'. However, apart from direct cruelty towards pets such as neglect and the use of 'pets' as fighting animals (for example the recent controversies over pit bull terriers), many feel that the whole notion of keeping animals as pets is ethically unsound.

i) Arguments in favour

- We can learn a great deal from and about animals when we keep them as pets – it helps us understand the animals and also develops our own good qualities – like care, kindness etc.
- If kept well, being a pet is hardly a hardship.
- Pets can be kept in environments which are very close to the state they would experience in the wild.
- Animals can actually benefit from being pets. They can receive a great deal of love and attention and can actually live 'better' lives than they would in the wild. Besides, many domestic pets have been bred for so long that they might be unable to survive without human help anyway.

ii) Arguments against

- Keeping an animal captive against its will cannot be justified.
- What right do we have to 'use' animals as educational tools for our own benefit?
- The life that any pet leads can rarely be compared to what it would experience in the wild.
- Many people are happy with their pets until they need money spent on them, or until they grow out of the 'cute' stage.

The issue here is the extent to which humans can and should control the lives of other living things, and also what can be learned. Critics of pet-keeping claim that the only thing that children learn when keeping pets is that humans are in charge, and that they have absolute control over another living being's life. Research seems to support the idea that many young people (often someone's major justification for keeping pets) learn few positive things about animals by keeping pets, rather they simply develop an overgrown sense of their own position in life. Supporters of keeping pets might argue that the relationship is symbiotic – it has benefits for the animal and for its owner, and that therefore it is perfectly acceptable and even desirable.

It is also often argued that only animals which have been domesticated are generally kept as pets – the real issue lies with the keeping of animals which are wild.

h) Zoos

Most modern zoos are far removed from what they used to be. There was a time when zoos sent hunters out to the wilds to capture and return animals for exhibit. Many abuses occurred. For example, it was common to kill females of a species so that their young could be captured alive. Adult animals were difficult to keep whereas young ones could adapt more easily to zoo life. In addition, it would be quite common for animals to be used in a 'performing' capacity; for example there were 'chimpanzees tea parties' where groups of chimps would be dressed up in human clothes, sat round a table and allowed to have a party. This would be much enjoyed by visitors. Finally, in the past zoos often made few attempts to make the animals' lives more bearable. Cages could be cramped, small, and arranged in such a way that the animals' lives would be very boring. Supporters of zoos would claim that these days are entirely over, whereas opponents might counter-claim that these practices have not entirely died out (with the probable exception that almost all zoos source their exhibits in an acceptable way). However, although many people still enjoy visits to the zoo, it is questionable how often they really think about the issues involved.

i) Arguments in favour

● They educate. People will be more concerned about wild populations of animals if they have been able to experience the real thing in a zoo – there is no substitute for experiencing the real thing. Science too can learn from such captive animals. This can enable scientific measures to be taken to preserve wildlife.

● They allow animal species to be preserved – many zoos engage in thorough breeding programmes. This means that wild populations will be able to be replenished from zoo animal stock

● Zoo animals can live perfectly fulfilling lives in a zoo. Enclosures are now very elaborate, reflect the wild environment, allow for animal socialisation, and prevent the animal from becoming bored or stressed

● Abuses of animals are prevented by strict legislation and the pressure of organisations such as 'Zoocheck' – as well as staff at zoos who are all keen on maintaining the welfare of the animals.

ii) Arguments against

● The educational value of zoos is minimal. Most people learn little. Instead they come away from the zoo more than ever confirmed in their prejudices that animals are funny, smelly and behave very oddly. They will be no more likely to support animals in the wild than they were before their visit to the zoo.

● No matter how elaborate and thoughtful an enclosure, it is still a prison. We do not have the right to keep animals in such false environments

● The amount of breeding which takes place in zoos is minimal, and certainly not enough to justify their existence. Additionally, the numbers of wild populations replenished by zoo-bred creatures is negligibly small. Besides which, animals bred from zoo-stock may not always be genetically varied enough or socially well-enough adjusted to survive a wild environment. So zoos do not play a significant role in preserving species.

● Despite stringent rules and regulations, serious abuses still occur.

In short, the existence of zoos today is firstly justified in terms of its educational value, and therefore its value in 'waking people up to' the realities of humanity's impact on the animal world. This will hopefully lead to overall improvements in the treatment of animals. Secondly it is justified as a valid scientific activity which helps us understand and improve the lives of animals, and helps us to put right previous wrongs.

One of the strongest justifications for the existence of zoos is probably the part that they might play in solving this concluding issue:

i) Biodiversity

> But why does it matter if the world loses a few strange plants and animals? It matters because extinction is forever. With those plants and animals, however strange and exotic, goes a slice of the world's genetic resource, a resource which ... keeps the world alive and habitable. It's got to stop, not just because we don't want our grandchildren to grow up in a world without gorillas, whales tigers and elephants, but because those genetic resources are of vital importance to all our futures.
>
> D Bellamy & B Quayle, *Turning the Tide*, p.150

Although Earth teems with life-forms, there is continual change in the relative numbers of species. The vast majority of living things which have roamed the Earth throughout its history do not do so today. As you read, species die out, reduce in number – and appear and increase in number. Everyone is familiar with the high profile extinctions like the Dodo, but fewer with the animals which theoretically died out following the meteor strike in the Yucatan peninsula millions of years ago. The fact that the rhino is endangered is well-known: in the 1970s there were probably around 72,000 in the wild, now there are less than 2,000. However, less well-known is that in the 70s there were estimated to be 30,000 sea-lions. Estimates put this figure at 180,000 today. It is true, however, that one of the most common environmental 'causes' you are likely to encounter today is one related to the maintaining of biodiversity. Usually these are centred upon a campaign to 'save the ...' it may be whale, dolphin, rhino or other animal species. Nothing taps the emotional well of green concern more readily than the attempt to save some species from the alleged damage done by another – and that villain almost always *Homo sapiens*.

There are not exactly arguments for and against here because people rarely state coldly that they are happy to see the end of some species or other. However, there are still opposing viewpoints. Viewpoints which support moves to preserve biodiversity might include the following:

- The variety of living things on Earth is good, and is in a state of delicate balance. Humans, considering that our power enables us to affect that balance out of proportion to our numbers, should act carefully to maintain that balance.
- The loss of species may have unforeseen consequences (for example, effects on the food chain or other natural cycles) which may actually be harmful to the human species – on the other hand, little understood species may hold benefits for humans or the planet which we do not fully understand at the moment. If we kill these species off we will never know what the benefits might have been.

- A world without the variety of species we have now would be a poorer place. It would be wrong if our actions now robbed our descendants of the joys of nature which we still enjoy
- All living things on Earth have a right to life for their own sake. Faced with the human onslaught, animals have few defences – we must make allowances for that by protecting them where we can.
- Extinction usually arises from inappropriate use of the animal world – humans must learn to cooperate rather than dominate

However, from the opposite side of the moral fence one could argue quite reasonably:

- Extinction is part of the normal process of life on Earth, in fact it is the mechanism by which life on Earth develops. If evolution has selected some species for extinction, even if that happens to be by our hands, then we must not interfere.
- Besides which, artificial interference in natural systems is notoriously difficult to control and should therefore be avoided. Natural extinction (however one defines that), tends to be good for life on Earth because it leaves 'gaps' which other species rapidly fill.
- The responsibility of humans is to their own species first. Where human existence comes into conflict with animals, human needs should come first – even if this regrettably means that certain species become extinct. So, for example, if certain fish species have become endangered and protecting them affects fishermen's livelihoods, what right have we to put people's lives at risk for our own sense of the aesthetically pleasing, or indeed our own interpretation of what is 'natural'.
- If humans play too dominant a role in the balance of species, nature will find its own way of putting the balance right again – though we might dislike the solution.

Maintaining biodiversity raises many other issues, as well as the more general question of the relationship between humans and animals. Humans have always considered their links with animals important and, whether it's the prehistoric hunter or contemporary research scientist, have developed ethical responses to the issues raised by this relationship.

6 Ethical responses

Having looked at the moral status of animals as well as specific issues related to their treatment, we will now consider how certain ethical traditions respond to the treatment and moral status (hence rights) of animals.

a) Altruism

i) Treatment of animals

Any mistreatment of an animal could be by definition, difficult for an altruist to accept. Altruism, remember, means putting the needs of others before your own. While many will limit this to humans, others may widen it to include animals. So for example, if an altruist believed that the eating of meat caused suffering to an animal, he might give it up – even if that involved sacrifice for himself. Unless altruism is limited to the human species – in which case any treatment of animals might be morally acceptable – as an altruist, one would have to treat animals fairly at least. The problem for the altruist would come when benefits conflicted. For example, if it could be shown that a painful and cruel experiment on an animal would almost certainly benefit many humans, then most altruists would have to accept the experiment. This could be seen as an evil – but a necessary one.

ii) Moral status

If animals are of lower worth than humans, then how we treat them is only a problem where that treatment will harm other humans. The altruist seeks the benefit of others, and if this is hindered by elevating animals to a higher moral status – where we would need to behave differently towards them – then that might be a problem. If the altruist extends his altruism to animals, then he will have to judge that their moral status should be the same as humans – so as to give them the protection from harm which we enjoy. This would then be acting in the animals' best interests. Again however, where there is conflict is where the problems will arise. For example, if someone was in the Arctic lost in a snowstorm, then it could be thought of as perfectly acceptable by the altruist for that person to kill an animal and use its fur for warmth. The key issue for the altruist therefore is the extent to which he can extend his altruistic behaviour beyond humans.

b) Egoism

i) Treatment of animals

The egoist is likely to say that any treatment of an animal is acceptable provided that it satisfies one's own self-interest. What counts as self-interest may be difficult to define in different situations, and may vary between individual egoists. For example, some egoists may support the use of veal crates because it produces the most enjoyable meat – their self-interest is satisfied through their stomachs. Other egoists might argue that the guilt felt while eating the meat will outweigh the benefits to your taste buds. The consequences of the action are important too. For example, one egoist might support factory farming because it produces a cheap and regular product. However, if this egoist could be persuaded that factory farming was more likely to produce a more dangerous product, then he might re-think his support for it. Self-interest can hardly be satisfied by a steak which has BSE written on it.

ii) Moral status

Again there are a variety of approaches which the egoist might take. If the status granted to an animal was likely to harm your own self-interest then that status would have to be questioned. This of course is the problem. It would have to be reasonably easy to predict what might be personally advantageous and what might not. For example, allowing the use of animals in medical research reflects society's belief that the general moral status of animals is lower than humans. Such research brings benefits, some life-saving – how could the egoist argue with that?

Some might. It could be argued that by exploiting an animal in this way we somehow 'eat into' our own humanity. This has the effect of diminishing us as a species and also individually. This could lead to arrogance, and ultimately to actions which go against your own self-interest. For example, some have argued that the easier it is for you to accept the death of one creature, the easier it might be to accept the death of others. Perhaps a society which treats animals badly is more likely to treat humans badly too. Such a scenario would be in no one's interest.

c) Legalism

i) Treatment of animals

The problem for the legalist is in deciding whether legally right and morally right are the same thing. For example, cruelty towards animals is illegal in Britain, however the transport of live animals to Europe is still legal – and many consider this very cruel. The legalist will have to reach his own decisions about the extent to which the law adequately covers what he otherwise believes to be right. He will also have to decide what to do about it if he thinks that a specific law is wrong! Laws reflect society as well as shape it. Someone who values the law wants to see it being appropriately set and monitored. In relation to the treatment of animals this is not always the case. For example, many legally unacceptable acts of cruelty towards animals carry very low fines. Also many legally acceptable 'acts of cruelty' are outside the scope of the law entirely. The complexity of the law is also a problem. For example, certain actions towards animals are perfectly legal in one country, but would be considered barbaric in others. Must therefore the legalist change his moral thinking should he move to live in another country – or while on holiday?

ii) Moral status

The trouble for the legalist is that there are very few clear statements anywhere in the world which define the moral status of animals. For example, in Britain, if your car hits a dog or a farm animal you must report it to the police – but not if you hit a rabbit or a bird. The law has to take many things into account when deciding if something is illegal. For example, if you beat your dog that would be illegal – but what about the jockey lashing his horse towards the finishing line? Legally there would appear to be contradictions about our thinking about animals. The bird in the conservation area seems valued, but not the one in the butcher's shop window.

d) Situation ethics

i) Treatment of animals

At the risk of repeating it all again, it depends on the situation. Situations vary, as do interpretations of the situation. What one person calls cruel, another calls natural. Fox hunting is a good example. Some say that it is cruel, others that it is a way of maintaining balance in the countryside. Environmentalists can also face difficult individual situations. For example, what if you found yourself as a conservationist who had to cull many of one species so that it did not kill off another? Many conservationists argue that it is acceptable to reduce one species in order to support another. In a different situation, a different response might be required.

ii) Moral status

This is a difficult area for the situation ethicist, because it is hard to argue that something's moral status changes according to the situation. Can a creature's intrinsic value change in different circumstances? It might seem logical not to believe so, but the situation ethicist can argue otherwise. While the moral status of an animal might not change, the extent to which we observe the requirements of that status might. Take an example, let us agree that a tiger has a certain moral status. This moral status does not vary whether the tiger is in the wild or in the circus. But say, for example, that a certain tiger is to be released from the circus back into the wild, after 15 years of circus life. Normally, the view that the tiger's moral status requires that it be allowed to go free would apply, but not in this situation. The tiger will have lost many of its survival skills, and so perhaps it is actually better in this situation to keep it in captivity. Even though it has the right to be free, that freedom might not be in its best interests. So although a thing's moral status might not vary, the situation ethicist might argue that the implications of that status can only be pursued in certain situations and not others.

e) Utilitarianism

i) Treatment of animals

Any treatment of animals is morally acceptable provided that it results in the greatest benefit for the greatest number. For example, killing cows with BSE might be cruel, but their deaths benefit many. However, the example of BSE strikes a warning note for the utilitarian more generally. It is suggested that BSE was caused by the feeding of ground up body parts from some animals to cows. This utilised otherwise unusable produce to make something edible. In classic utilitarian terms this could have been seen to make much sense. The benefit of the many at little real cost to anyone. However, this practice backfired, resulting in BSE and the human version CJD, which clearly does not maximise happiness for the greatest number. The utilitarian will argue therefore that how we treat animals has to be carefully considered, because the outcome of that treatment should benefit the many. This outcome is not always obvious – as many argue in the case of certain scientific experiments, for example.

ii) Moral status

Similarly, the utilitarian must be sure that the status given to animals does not disadvantage the happiness of the many. For example, if animal experiments were all outlawed tomorrow on the grounds that animals were to have the same rights as humans, then perhaps many cures and treatments would never be discovered. This would obviously result in drawbacks for the many. The utilitarian would need to be clear that any change in our thinking about the moral status of animals was actually going to produce the greatest benefit for the greatest number – there is no other motivation.

f) Religious authority

As in many areas of environmental ethics, many of today's views are based upon the historical teachings of Christianity. What follows should give you an outline of this teaching.

i) The Biblical view

Christians believe that the Bible gives mankind dominion over the animal world. This dominion is to be exercised in two ways:

- Using animals as necessary – for food and as helps in life's tasks
- Providing conditions for life in which animals may thrive.

Christians also believe that a major theme in the Bible is the protection of the weak by the strong. Many argue that this should be the guiding principle as far as the relationship between humans and animals is concerned.

There are strict regulations in the Bible about how animals are to be treated. Many argue that this is contradictory. For example, animals are allowed to rest on the Sabbath Day, but animals could be sacrificed to celebrate special occasions. There is dispute too about whether animals were meant to be eaten. In the earliest Genesis stories, it seems to suggest that vegetarianism is what God wants – but after the fall story it seems as if animals are to walk in dread of humans. What is not clear in the Biblical material is how far animals have intrinsic or instrumental value. Many of the teachings seem to suggest that animals have worth only so far as they benefit humans. However, the inclusion of 'two of every species' in the flood story seems to suggest a God who was concerned for the welfare of animals for their own sake.

The problem of course is that the Bible does not deal with specific modern issues like xenotransplantation and animal experiments. Christians have to study the general themes of how the Bible refers to animals and then try to apply that teaching to more specific contemporary issues. Animals clearly have value both for humans and for God, but how far that value can be eroded when humans are in conflicting moral situations with respect to animals is unclear from the Biblical material alone. There is certainly a prime place given to humans over animals, but many Christians disagree about how absolute this is.

ii) Theological development
Much of what modern Christianity believes about animals is derived from the interpretations of the Bible made in the Middle Ages by Thomas Aquinas. He argued that:

- Animals, being without souls, were lesser beings than humans. How they were treated therefore didn't matter.
- Animals exist for the use of mankind alone.
- They have no rights because they do not share our nature.
- Humans therefore have no responsibility towards them.

> In the theology of Aquinas ... the process of redemption applied to humans ... but not other creatures. Such theology emphasised the lack of rationality in animals and paved the way for subsequent beliefs which reinforced their low status. This freed people from sensing guilt and fear that they were causing suffering ... They reasoned that either animals did not feel pain, or if they did, that this was of no concern to God.
>
> Tim Cooper, *Green Christianity*, p.224

iii) Current thinking
Andrew Linzey is perhaps the most prominent thinker within Christianity on animal issues. He argues:

● Animals have rights because they belong to God (he calls this 'theos-rights').
● There is a requirement on humans to protect the weak – animals can be considered weak.
● Dominion implies first of all responsibility not domination.
  Free will is important. Animals cannot exercise their free will in relation to how they would like to be treated. It is wrong of us to take advantage of this just because we can.

The idea that the specifically animal creation should be the subject of honour and respect because it is created by God ... is not one that has been given endorsement throughout centuries of Christian thought ... whilst it is true that many saints, sages, divines and poets within [Christianity] have shown or articulated respect for animals, the idea remains largely vague and unfocused.

Andrew Linzey, *Animal Theology*, p.3

7 Conclusion

The common thread throughout all these issues is the extent to which animals should be attributed the same rights as humans. If they are worthy of the same rights as us then this obviously has implications for the ways in which we allow them to be treated. It is quite clear that animals are in a position of weakness relative to humans, and also that they are unable to respond to things in a way that we would be able to understand. This means that we have to look closely at our relationship with animals because by definition it is unequal. We are 'strong' and they are relatively 'weak'. It is almost universally agreed that the strong should support the weak – perhaps this might be one of the overall guiding principles we apply in this topic.

However, this has to take into account the possibility that we should always seek the maximum good for the greatest number of people (or indeed living things) and that sometimes this might involve conflicts of interest. Much of the debate in this topic surrounds just these conflicts of interest and how they might be solved. The problem, some would argue, is that in the case of animals, the human species has to act as judge and jury as well as defendant and prosecution, not to mention key witness. The animal world is ethically mute – so we must take that responsibility on. Inevitably such a role produces a wide variety of views.

The issue of the complexity of the treatment and rights of animals is important too. Also, as in other areas of environmental ethics, there is the problem of unpredictability of outcome.

Study guides

You should build your study notes around the following headings:

- What rights should animals have?
- In what ways are animals well or poorly treated in society today – and what issues does this treatment raise?
- What arguments are used to support better treatment for animals?
- How are these arguments opposed?
- What rights over animals should humans have?
- Where does the authority for this come from?
- How do ethical traditions respond to animal issues?
- How does Christian teaching respond to these same issues?
- What are your own conclusions on the issue of animal rights generally and on the specific issues raised in this chapter?

You should remember that each of the issues has at least two sides to it and you should be able to argue both of them convincingly. You should also be able to use examples to support your view or to refute the opposite view. You should also bear in mind that the nature of ethics means that even within ethical systems there are bound to be conflicts – so, for example, it would be difficult to state that there is 'a Christian view'. In any essay on this topic you would be expected to show that you are aware of the conflicts between and within different ethical responses. You should make sure too, that you can critically analyse a viewpoint – whether you agree with it or not.

Questions in this area are likely to ask you to do the following:

- Identify an issue.
- Outline the scientific background to the issue.
- Outline a range of ethical responses to this issue, often directly related to the background material you are demonstrating your grasp of.
- Weigh up the relative merits of these responses, pitting them against each other where appropriate.
- (Often) Give your own reasoned conclusion about the issue based on your own synthesis and analysis of a variety of viewpoints and ethical stances.
- (Or) Come to a conclusion about which ethical response replies most appropriately to the issue raised.

The balance of any examination answer here is likely to be decided by the question. However, there is a general rule for any ethical study, particularly in relation to issues which fall into the category of science. The exam is not just a test of what you remember but a test of how well you can apply that knowledge. The examiner does not want you to repeat your teacher's notes but to give your own account of what you have studied and learned. There is a balance to be struck between the descriptive and the evaluatory. An answer which was pure description would receive few marks – it needs to be picked apart, analysed, debated and discussed, and occasionally concluded upon. It needs to treat the background as just that, the peg upon which you hang your argument. In short, an answer including 100 facts and five points of discussion which is twenty pages long might do less well than one including thirty facts and fifteen points of discussion ten pages long.

For any exam question you should ask yourself if you have:

- included all the relevant background information
- included all the relevant ethical responses
- analysed and evaluated these responses in light of the question set.

Each question is different but good practice usually involves:

Describing, Analysing, Evaluating, Concluding – Relevantly

Sample Essay Question and Guide

'To what extent are zoos important in preserving animal species?'

1. Describe the principles and practices of the modern zoo – perhaps with passing reference to improvements made in recent years.
2. Consider the ways in which zoos might preserve wildlife:
   - Increase public awareness – so help shift public attitudes in favour of preservation
   - Breeding programmes preserve DNA stocks of endangered species
   - Wild populations can therefore be re-stocked from zoo-bred animals
   - Zoo breeding is free from the threats (human and animal) of the wild and can be controlled in desirable directions
   - Zoos enable scientific research which is not always feasible in the wild environment – helps scientists devise techniques to support preservation.
3. Consider criticisms of these contentions:
   - Zoos do little to educate, so no gain in interest on part of public for preservation
   - Zoo bred animals not genetically fit for the wild
   - Little real breeding takes place in zoos, and then often only 'valuable' species not endangered ones
   - Zoos enable humans to avoid the real issue – preserving nature in the wild
4. Choose as many of these as time/knowledge allows and analyse them by comparing them and supporting/ rejecting them as you see fit.

5. Weigh up the arguments and begin to highlight the most powerful ones in your opinion and explain why you think they are powerful.
6. Summarise your most relevant points and conclude. This question is asking you 'To what extent' which also means 'how far'. You have the following options, one of which you should run with consistently.

Option 1 – Zoos are very important in preserving animal species
Option 2 – Zoos are important in some ways in preserving animal species
Option 3 – Zoos are irrelevant to the preservation of animal species
Option 4 – Zoos are harmful to the preservation of animal species

You have to decide on your own weighting for your point of view, though it is always important to stress that there are many interpretations of this statement. Even if you take a very strong line one way or the other you must show that you are aware of a variety of viewpoints on the topic – that is what analysis and evaluation is after all.

Remember too that throughout your answer you should consider the implications of various philosophical viewpoints concerning the moral status of animals.

Typical Exam Questions

1. 'The testing of drugs on animals is a necessary cruelty.' To what extent do you agree with this statement?
2. 'Vegetarianism is not natural.' Discuss.
3. To what extent is fox-hunting still acceptable today?
4. 'The factory farm is an economic necessity.' How far might a Christian support this statement?
5. 'Keeping any animal captive is morally wrong.' Discuss.
6. 'Humans have a special responsibility for animals.' To what extent do you agree?

Activities and Discussion Points

This is an area which lends itself well to debate. This will involve a fair degree of research on the part of individual members of the class. You should mix formal debating with more informal. It is also an area where the contribution of outside speakers will be valuable – this can be done in a 'question time' format. For the more media-conscious, the preparation and presentation of mock news items and short magazine 'articles' will enable you to explore the issues more fully, especially as they relate to the environment around you. Small-scale research projects are valuable here too. This can range from explorations of local animal issues, or just general 'market research' about opinions on the use/abuse of animals.

Suggestions for Further Reading

1. *The Status of Animals*: Paterson & Palmer (Ed), CAB, 1989
   ISBN 0 85198 650 1
2. *Animal Theology*: A Linzey, SCM, 1994, ISBN 0334 00005 X
3. *In Defence of Animals*: P Singer (Ed), Blackwell, 1985,
   ISBN 0 631 13897 8
4. *Man and the Natural World*: K Thomas, Allen Lane, London, 1983,
5. *Animal Rights*: Henry Salt, Centaur Press, Sussex, 1980
6. *The Case for Animal Rights*: Tom Regan, UCLA Press, Berkely, 1984
7. *Engineering Genesis*: D & A Bruce (Eds) Earthscan, 1998,
   ISBN 1 85383 570 6
8. *Green Christianity*: T Cooper; Hodder & Stoughton, 1990,
   ISBN 0 340 52339 5
9. *Turning the Tide*: D Bellamy & B Quayle; Collins, 1986,
   ISBN 0 00 219368 X

4 The Human Dimension

1 Introduction

KEY ISSUES
- To what extent does the range and number of humans on Earth pose issues for the environment?
- What are the causes and effects of poverty?
- To what extent is there economic justice in the world?
- How far is it the responsibility of developed countries to help developing ones?
- What issues are involved in human population growth?
- What might be the environmental consequences of development?
- How do various ethical traditions respond to these issues?

Strange that two thirds of the world are starving while the other third is slimming.

quoted in D Bellamy & B Quayle, *Turning the Tide*, p.13

By now you should be in little doubt about the power and influence of the human species on Earth. What about relationships within the human species? As you explored the previous issues, you will have become aware that many environmental issues have a dimension which is related to our own growth and development as humans. You saw that many environmental problems may be caused by human demand for some product or other – for example, the need for energy which cannot always be met in a sustainable way. Human needs and wants often involve conflict between what is beneficial for us and what is good for the environment. Human society is always growing and always changing. Everything that we do has the potential to leave its mark on nature. The likelihood is that this will continue for some time to come.

There are two main reasons why the issues you are about to examine are important:

- Humans are part of the environment. One of the most common mistakes is to think that 'the environment' is something which is somehow 'outside' humanity. It is not. Humans are part of it, and everything we do has consequences for it. Also, whatever we do to the natural world affects us too.

  One common environmental theme is the idea of interconnectedness, that all things are bound together in chains of cause and effect. You have seen how this can be the case in relation to pollution, which is just as likely to harm human society as the animal world or the systems of the Earth. Even breathing has environmental impact, and it is unavoidable. What most environmentalists aim to expose are those instances where our environmentally harmful actions are avoidable.

- Being part of the environment, our actions affect it. The difference between humans and other living things is that we can consciously choose to do something about it. Human intellectual ability means that we can study cause and effect, make reasonable predictions and alter our behaviour so that what we judge to be harmful situations may improve. This ability to critically reflect on our actions and change them appropriately is significant. As far as we know, no other species does this, or at least no other species can do it to the extent that we can. Humans can modify nature to a significant extent – for good or ill. However, when so much of our energy is devoted to improving our own lifestyles, the result can be inequalities in the system elsewhere, either for nature or for other humans who are a part of it.

Currently, human society is categorised in three ways (though many prefer to link the developing and the underdeveloped world into one category – which is what this chapter will do). Interaction between these three categories is often regarded as the underlying cause of many of the issues you are about to explore:

- The developed world – sometimes referred to as the 'first world', these countries are wealthy and powerful. Life expectancy is high and education, social welfare and healthcare is good. These countries tend to base their economies on industry. Standards of living are usually high with most people able to enjoy luxury products, as well as meet their basic needs comfortably.
- The developing world – these countries are in transition, in other words are becoming developed countries. Standards of living, including the social indicators referred to above, are fair. These countries tend to be in the process of industrialising. Many people are able to enjoy luxuries, although greater numbers live more basic existences.
- The underdeveloped world – these countries usually have little industry and poor standards of living. Many people's incomes are only able to provide for their basic needs, and there are significant numbers who live in poverty. Life expectancy is low and social standards are poor. These countries are often heavily in debt to the developed nations.

NB This chapter will use 'developing world' to include 'underdeveloped' and 'developing' as above.

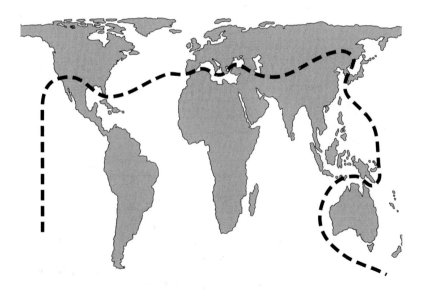

The North-South divide

The division between the developed and the developing world is often referred to as the North–South divide. This is because, geographically most developed nations are in the North whereas most developing nations are in the South.

> The North: The industrialised countries provide for most of their inhabitants a relatively easy life. Almost everyone has access to clean water, sanitation, clothes and primary health care. Almost everyone can eat to their satisfaction …
>
> The South: … [eg] Sub-Saharan Africa; More than half the population have no access to public health services; two-thirds lack safe water; 18 million people suffer from sleeping sickness; malaria kills thousands of children every year … and in the poorest countries a quarter or more of the children die before the age of five.
>
> United Nations Report, *A Vision of Hope*, 1995, p.123 & 129

To say that a nation is developed already involves certain ethical judgments. Quality of life is often difficult to measure, and it could well be argued that life in a community which is materially poor but 'emotionally rich' is better than life in a faceless big city where material possessions are plentiful – though others might view this as naive idealism.

Also some variations are likely. For example, Cuba would be labelled a developing nation, where many would be considered to be poor by developed world standards. However, the regime there seems to ensure that standards of education and healthcare are extremely high – better in fact than in many developed nations. Also in many Middle Eastern oil-rich countries there is still a great deal of poverty.

You may have noticed already the extent to which environmental issues can be thought of as issues of competition. Competing demands for resources, space to live and ways of life can be subjects of competition between humans, as well as between the human species and other living things. Much of what follows results directly from that notion of competition. Many would claim that this is perfectly natural and therefore outside the scope of ethics. Others might suggest that the human ability to modify its behaviour implies that we should.

As you explore the issues which follow, be aware that many of them already imply certain values over others, and that ethically, the right or wrong course of action in each situation is not simple, nor always obvious. In the same way that the specific environmental issues were complex scientifically, these issues are equally complex socially, economically and politically.

2 Poverty

> Next to birth, the chief cause of success in life is accident and opportunity.
>
> JS Mill, *Utilitarianism*, p.216

> Poverty is a great enemy to human happiness; it certainly destroys liberty, and it makes some virtues impracticable and others extremely difficult.
>
> Samuel Johnson (1709–84)

a) What is poverty?

The instinctive answer is that poverty is when you have no money and cannot have what you want. A more developed answer might be that it is where you are unable to secure the things that you need to survive. MD Morris, in 1975, came up with the concept of the 'Physical Quality of Life Index' (PQLI) which includes life expectancy, infant mortality and adult literacy rates. This is one approach to measuring poverty. Another is calorie supply as a percentage of requirements – i.e. whether you have enough food or not. However, what it means to be poor may still differ depending upon your point of view.

i) Relative poverty

This is where we can compare one person's wealth with another. For example, in any group of people in the UK some will be paid more than others; some will have larger debts than others; some will own homes and cars and so on. In relation to each other we are relatively poor or wealthy. The level of our poverty therefore depends upon whom we compare ourselves with. If most people in the UK were to compare themselves to many in the developing world, they might find that to be British is to be very wealthy. For example, GNP per capita in the UK is around US$ 8460, in Ethiopia, US$110. This means simply that the average person in the UK is around 76 times wealthier than the average Ethiopian. Relative poverty may be a problem within countries as economic divisions foster social unrest. It is less obvious between countries.

ii) Absolute poverty

> Poverty at the absolute level … is life at the very margin of existence. The absolute poor are severely deprived human beings struggling to survive in a set of squalid and degraded circumstances almost beyond the power of our sophisticated imaginations and privileged circumstances to conceive.
>
> Robert McNamara, Former President of the World Bank quoted in P Singer, *Practical Ethics*, p.219

The Worldwatch Institute defines absolute poverty as 'the lack of sufficient income in cash or kind to meet the most basic biological needs for food, clothing and shelter'. This is poverty where lack of purchasing power can threaten your very existence. There are those in absolute poverty in every country of the world, though far greater numbers and proportions in the developing world. In the developed world we tend to express this as 'living below the poverty (or bread) line'.

> The World Bank estimates that 1.3 billion people live in absolute poverty, with incomes of less than $1 a day or less.'
>
> LR Brown, *State of the World*, p.119

Absolute poverty is of major ethical concern because it presents challenges for our social, economic and political structures worldwide – as well as a significant moral challenge.

b) Causes and effects of poverty

i) Place
Individual poverty is most often directly linked to the economic status of the country in which you live. In the UK for example, even if you earn very little you are still entitled to free healthcare as often as you require. This is because people in economically stable and prosperous countries are able to subsidise those who, for whatever reason, are not able to meet the costs of their own basic needs. People in Scandinavian countries for example, are heavily taxed – but everyone there enjoys the very high standards of social provision which these taxes permit. If you happen to live in a poorer country your ability to improve your economic lot will be limited by the state of your country generally, often regardless of how hard you work.

ii) The means of production
You can only become wealthy if you are able to create wealth, and this can best be done where you can control the means of production. Put simply there's little advantage in sitting on a gold mine if you don't own mining equipment. Karl Marx identified capitalists as those who controlled the means of production. Individuals could sell their labour to these capitalists, but without control of the means of production these individuals would remain relatively poor. Poor countries may lack the capital to purchase the means of production, and may therefore allow wealthier countries to exploit their natural resources. Alternatively poor countries may borrow from wealthy countries in order to pay for capital equipment. This means that the country begins its economic development in a state of debt which itself limits the creation of wealth.

iii) Other specific factors

Across the world and in individual countries there are widely varying degrees of poverty. The nature of society, as it is presently, ensures that some are better off than others. Each country has its share of poor and wealthy – often living closely, as each depends on the other for different aspects of their existence. There are different points of view about how someone becomes rich and others remain poor. The reality of the matter is probably a combination of the following:

- hard work and effort – many would suggest that one of the principal reasons why someone is wealthy is that they have worked to get that way. In the developed world there is often a strong link suggested between how hard you work and how successful you become. This 'work ethic' has led many to conclude that poverty is a mark of lack of effort. Unfortunately, such a view can blind those who are successful to the plight of others who may not be poor because they don't work hard enough.
- luck – many might argue that becoming wealthy is a case of 'being in the right place at the right time'. Chance may present you with an opportunity which you can capitalise on so as to improve your standard of life. Many would claim that this is in fact the key – many people work extremely hard, but manage only to survive, whereas others simply get 'the breaks'.
- benefits of previous wealth or poverty – many people of course are poor or wealthy because their parents were. Often these cycles are broken – for example where someone from a poor background 'makes good', or someone from a wealthy background 'falls on hard times'. At any rate, there is usually a connection down the generations, as the effort or good fortune of parents is passed on to their children.

iv) Effects

What is certainly the case is that poverty involves consequences. For example, someone living in poverty in the UK today is far more likely than someone wealthy to:

- end up in prison
- suffer ill-health
- die prematurely
- follow a poor dietary regime
- do badly in school and not go on to higher education
- be unemployed.

Poverty is not just the absence of money, but a set of social circumstances which are both directly harmful and likely to lead to further poverty. Some have referred to this a vicious downward spiral, because with each slip downwards it becomes more and more difficult to work your way back up again.

In the developing world, the effects of poverty are usually far more severe. Here, someone living in poverty is more likely to:

- suffer from malnutrition and ultimately literally die of starvation
- suffer serious long-term ill-health
- be tied to poor working conditions – often a form of slavery
- have to engage in de-humanising activities which ensure survival, for example, prostitution, or the selling or abandoning of children
- put children to work in poor and unsafe conditions.

In the developed world, however, instances of absolute poverty are far fewer than in the developing world because developing countries as a whole tend to be poor.

c) National poverty

What does it mean to say that a country is poor?

The world economy is very complex. Countries may be rich in resources, in labour, in skills, and in all sorts of ways and yet remain poor. Though this might seem odd there are reasons why this may be the case.

- A country may be rich in resources but lack the industrial machinery or means of production to make use of these resources adequately.
- Powerful and wealthy countries may therefore exploit those who are unable to make best use of their natural resources, for example, by pricing the means of production so high that poorer countries become dependent upon practical and financial support from richer countries. These countries may also control world markets so that the poorer countries have difficulties in selling their products at a reasonable profit.
- Small groups of wealthy elites may control the means of production in a country, failing to distribute the benefits widely. In many poor countries, those in such positions are often those left over from a country's colonial days.
- The infrastructure of a country may be unable to support economic development.
- Many poor countries start from a position of being in debt.

The importance of national poverty is significant. Where a country is poor it will be less able to create the right kind of conditions which would enable its people to prosper – another vicious downward spiral.

d) Economic injustice and inequality

i) International debt

In 1997, Comic Relief raised £26 million. This was paid back by Africa in debt repayments in just over a day.

Jubilee 2000 campaign

Debt relief by the year 2000 could save the lives of 21 million children.

Human Development Report, UNDP 1997

Most of the developing world is in debt. This debt is the result of borrowing which developing countries have engaged in so that they can industrialise. The International Monetary Fund (IMF) and the World Bank usually oversee these debts, though loans are also made directly from a developed nation to a developing one. Obviously these debts require to be repaid. There are two elements to this: repayment of the original capital and interest payments. The amounts are fairly staggering. For many developing countries, the repayment of their debt may involve around 85 per cent of the country's GNP each year. The implications of this are profound:

- developing countries have to devote much of their country's production to the export market. In order to pay debt, these countries require foreign currency. The only way to get this is by selling goods in overseas markets. This of course, means that these countries inevitably have to put the needs of their own people after the need to secure such funds in order to pay off their debts. For example, there is an emphasis on export (cash) crops instead of crop production to meet the needs of the country's own population. This is one of the principal reasons why, even though many developing nations are fertile and well-endowed with natural resources, the people who live in these countries sometimes benefit little from this.

Debt interest payments as a % of total exports

Uganda, 25.6; Ivory Coast, 15.1; Burundi 12.9; Bolivia, 16.9; Nicaragua 15.9.

World Development report, World Bank 1994

- this has wide implications. For example, these countries are unable to invest in their own infrastructure – so their ability to industrialise is further depleted. Also, so great a concentration on servicing this debt means that investment within the country takes second place in other ways too. Healthcare, education and other types of social provision are the inevitable casualties.
- there are also criticisms however. Many developing nations spend significant amounts of the GNP left over from debt repayment on military costs, and there is often widespread public and private corruption. However, this also occurs in developed nations, without the additional burden of debt repayments to be met.

International debt is a significant factor in world poverty. In short it means that if you are born in a developing nation, you are born into debt, and a proportion of your working life will be spent paying this debt off.

The Jubilee 2000 campaign aims to persuade the world's powerful nations to suspend the debts of many developing countries It suggests that rich countries should agree to a cancellation of what remains of developing world debt before the year 2000.

However, the need for a developing country to pay off its debts is often offset by international aid schemes – themselves sources of great controversy.

ii) Aid programmes

Rich nations take back £9 in debt for every £1 given in aid.

Global Development Finance 98

In recent years, the international community has provided fewer resources to support poorer countries. We want to reverse that trend. We are committed to increasing the amount of money we spend on development and in future all the assistance we give to developing countries will be in the form of grants not loans.

UK Government white paper, *Eliminating World Poverty: A Challenge for the 21st Century*, 1998

Charities and individuals assist those in poverty in the developing world, but our focus here is on the actions of the international community. Aid may come in the form of direct financial assistance, investment in a developing nation, direct goods and services, or professional and technical help in developing an infrastructure which enables the country to improve itself.

The United Nations has set a target for the world's developed countries. It suggests that each developed nation should aim to give 0.7 per cent of its GNP as aid to developing countries. None meet this target and many give considerably less. In fact, many developed nations are in the process of cutting back their aid programmes.

Overseas Development Assistance (ODA) is the way in which rich countries officially help poor ones. There is a distinction made by many between what might be considered appropriate aid and inappropriate aid. ODA is not without its problems:

● Much of it comes with conditions ('tied aid'). This may be that it is spent in a certain way, for example, in buying goods from the country which has donated it. It may also be specified for use in debt servicing. Some have suggested that this is simply an example of developed nations recycling their own funds. These conditions often come in the form of Structural Adjustment Programmes (SAPs). This involves the receiving country in agreeing to certain conditions for a loan. It generally requires the countries to make changes which, it is argued, will ultimately ease their economic difficulties. SAPs for example, may require the country to:

- cut its spending on social services
- change from subsistence to cash crop production
- attract overseas investment through incentive schemes.
- The ODA may not actually benefit the people of the country concerned. Apart from the changes which SAPs require, it has long been argued that ODA merely keeps poor countries dependent upon the richer ones, and simply makes these countries more vulnerable to exploitation. The inhabitants of the country see little benefit – instead, one form of slavery is replaced by another, as these countries have to bend to the will of the developed nations before receiving their 'rewards'.

It is clear that despite actions to balance the economic state of human society, poverty and economic imbalance remains:

the unmet needs are vast:

- 800 million people go to bed hungry every day.
- Nearly 900 million adults still cannot read or write.
- 1.5 billion people have no access to primary healthcare.
- 1.75 billion people are without safe water.
- 100 million people are completely homeless.
- A billion people eke out the barest existence in perpetual poverty.
- 40 million newborn children are not properly immunized. Fourteen million die every year before they reach the age of five and 150 million are malnourished.'

United Nations Report, *A Vision of Hope*, 1995

e) The environmental impact of poverty

... a child born in Britain, America or France this year will consume, waste and pollute more in a lifetime that 50 children in developing nations. But the one billion people in developing countries who have the least stake in the consumer society will bear the brunt of environmental damage. They tend to burn traditional fuels, use leaded petrol or live near factories and rubbish dumps.

The Electronic Telegraph, 10 September 1998

- Poverty may lead ultimately to social unrest, especially where someone's poverty is so abject that they feel they have nothing to lose. Wars and civil strife produce their own directly harmful environmental impact.
- The poverty of a nation may lead its government to take 'short cuts' with respect to the environment. Where the priority is securing foreign currency, environmental side-effects of industry or agriculture may be ignored. Also poor countries are more likely to over-exploit their natural resources in an unsustainable way – the pressure on the country's economy ultimately being far greater than the desire to conserve the natural world.

- Poor countries may also be exploited by rich ones as a result. For example, many poor countries may be willing to receive pollutants from wealthier ones in order to receive financial benefits. Also poorer countries may 'turn a blind eye' to environmentally suspect practices engaged in by industries which are foreign-owned, because of the revenue which these industries provide.
- Additionally, many poor countries may be willing to conserve nature, but be unable to do so. The equipment and expertise needed to protect the environment may not be within these countries' economic reach. Governments may not feel justified in diverting funds away from measures designed to alleviate their peoples' poverty in order to preserve the environment.

Many of these factors have led some rich nations to suggest that, given that the environment is a global issue, poorer countries should be helped to ensure that their development does not have harmful environmental impact. For example, in order to gain foreign currency, some poorer countries have felt it necessary to exploit their tropical rainforests. These are considered to be sites of world importance environmentally. Some rich countries have taken the view that aid to such countries should be dependent upon those countries preserving these rainforests. Thus, economic assistance becomes dependent upon managing the environment in a sustainable way.

This may leave many of these poor countries wondering why they should have to forego the economic benefits of exploiting their own natural resources – especially as in doing so they increase their dependence on aid from the developed world. This balance between economic development and environmental preservation is one of the key factors in this area.

3 Development issues

Why does international development matter? ... First because we have a moral duty to the poor and needy to try to create a more just world. Second, it's in all our interests. Global warming, polluted oceans, disappearing forests, shortage of fresh water, more and more mouths to feed ... these things affect us all ... without sustainable development we will never be able to eliminate poverty.

UK Government white paper, *Eliminating Poverty:*
A Challenge for the 21st Century

a) Economic development

The issue here is the extent to which a country should forego its own economic development in order to preserve the environment. Inevitably, this involves conflict, including questions as to the extent to which development is right and necessary, and also what 'price' may reasonably be placed upon it. The key to the conflict is often this: developed nations have begun to realise the negative environmental impact of their own economic development, though they enjoy the benefits of this development. They are concerned, however, that as developing nations go through the same processes, the environmental impact will be so serious as to affect the world as a whole. So the issue is how far developing nations can (or may be permitted to) develop economically before they begin to make the same mistakes which the developed world already has.

Perhaps the best example of this tension is the development of China. China is the fastest developing nation in the world. The world's most heavily populated country is moving rapidly from a rural, pre-industrial economy to an urban industrial one. With such rapid development attempting to meet the needs of such a vast population, many have suggested that environmental concerns have taken a very definite back seat, the 3 Gorges dam project being one example already mentioned. However, others have taken the view that economic development is a reality not an option, and that it is patronising and ultimately foolish to suggest that it should be halted or slowed down:

> The lives of Chinese villagers I know are infinitely better now than they were 30 years ago … China has become more open partly because of the demands of ordinary people. They want to become part of the world … People want refrigerators, stereos, CD players. I feel it's a moral obligation not to say: 'Those people out there should continue to live in a museum while we will have showers that work.'
>
> James Watson, Harvard anthropologist quoted in *National Geographic*
> August 1999, p.13

China, for example, has set itself the target of every household having its own refrigerator as soon as possible, and not necessarily one which is CFC-free.

The issue is quite clear. Economic development brings environmental challenge. How far should that development be undertaken with environmental concerns in mind? It has been pointed out that economic development, although it brings potential harm for the environment, also brings considerable benefit for people. After all, the same development which brings polluting industry may also bring clean water, sanitation and improved healthcare. Do the developed nations have the right to deny developing ones the benefits which those in the developed world already enjoy?

i) The challenge of industrialisation

Industrialisation is generally considered the key to improving the lives of a country's inhabitants. Most developing nations seek to industrialise, because with it may come improved healthcare, sanitation, infrastructure and so on. These direct benefits are in addition to the benefits to be had indirectly from living in a country which is economically stable – and so better able to provide for its population in all manner of ways. As industrial development brings economic improvement, it also creates improvement in quality of life generally. At least, this is the theory. There is disagreement about the extent to which a country's industrial and economic development will actually benefit its population. Many point out that there is often a difficult period to be gone through as the country takes its first steps towards industrialisation, and unless these stages of development are carefully managed, they can become permanently negative features of a newly developed country. For example, while development brings benefits there are also drawbacks:

- Industrialisation brings pollution. Before they have the economic strength to deal with this, many developing countries may find it unmanageable. This can have implications far wider than for just the country itself.
- Industrialisation brings social change. People's lifestyles change, and there is migration from rural to urban areas. This may produce tensions for those left behind (often wives and children) and for those who move (often husbands). The nature of communities change as a result. Urban environments may be more likely to develop other unwelcome social changes – for example increased drug misuse, violence and other social problems.
- Working conditions are often poor at first. As a country industrialises, working conditions may often take second place to the need to create wealth. There are many instances in the developing world of child labour, for example. There are also often those who have been called 'debt slaves' – people who in order to repay a debt offer to work it off instead – this work often continuing without limit.
- Women also find that they may have particularly difficult roles in a developing nation.

Generally speaking, newly developing nations may face similar kinds of problems to those faced in the UK during the industrial revolution of the 19th century.

b) Agricultural development

The UN Food & Agriculture Organisation, using national nutritional surveys, estimates that 841 million people living in developing countries suffer from basic protein-energy malnutrition.

LR Brown, *State of the World*, p.117

As the human population increases so does the need to feed it. Human food supply is, according to many commentators, one of the most pressing ethical and environmental issues today.

i) World hunger
On a planet which has sent men to the moon, famines still occur, much as they have throughout human history.

The camera wandered amidst them like a mesmerised observer, occasionally dwelling on one person so that he looked directly at me, sitting in my comfortable living room surrounded by the fripperies of modern living which we were pleased to regard as necessities. Their eyes looked into mine. There was an emaciated woman too weak to do anything but limply hold her dying child. There was a skeletal man holding out a bundle wrapped in sacking so that it could be counted; it looked like a tightly wrapped package of old sticks, but it was the desiccated body of his child ... All around was the murmur of death, like a hoarse whisper, or the buzzing of flies.

Bob Geldof, *Is That It?*, p.270

It would seem that as human population increases, more go hungry. Many commentators suggest that the Earth can sustain far greater population growth, provided that agricultural practice adjusts appropriately. There are many suggestions as to why many still quite literally starve to death:

- Developing countries export their food crops to raise foreign currency rather than feeding their own. During the Ethiopian famine in the 1980s, Ethiopia was still exporting vast quantities of food to the developed world.
- Developing countries often use their agricultural land to grow cash crops (e.g. tea, tobacco etc). This means that such land is unavailable for subsistence agriculture.
- 'Freak' events may cause crop failure. Developing nations are often unable to adapt to these circumstances because of their need to export their produce, and because of their poor infrastructure.
- Local troubles as well as local corruption often lead to the mismanagement of agricultural land.

Also, agricultural practice is becoming more technologically oriented. Farmers may find that to maintain production at the levels required, they have to invest in complex machinery, elaborate chemicals, specific seed-stocks. All of these cost money (and their production and distribution is usually controlled by developed nations). Without the capital to invest in such items, developing world farmers may find that their productivity decreases, and so they are unable to meet the needs of their own people. What may often happen here is that large agri-businesses from the developed world may move in and take over such land. These agri-businesses, often branches of multi-national corporations, are able to provide the necessary capital in order to make the necessary productive returns. Unfortunately, local people are then unable to buy the produce at the cost it has now assumed.

Therefore, in terms of world hunger, the issue is not one merely of supply and demand. Every year sees increases in food production worldwide, yet still many die of starvation and malnutrition. The issue instead is one of distribution and access. There is enough food, the problem is that it is unevenly – many would state unfairly – distributed. This equates with economic power. In short, the more economically developed a nation is, the less likely its people are to go hungry, as such nations can control the supply and distribution of food.

> ... hunger itself is a cause of poverty ... a constraint to economic and social development. Hunger and poverty have a two-way relationship. They feed off each other ... Hunger is the first threshold to cross on the way out of poverty ... there can be no growth without overcoming today's hunger.
>
> World Food Programme, 1997

c) The environmental impact of development

The environmental impacts of industry have already been discussed in the previous chapter. However, population growth and agricultural development both present significant environmental difficulties.

i) Population growth

In 1800, the world's population was about 900 million, by 1950, 2,500 million. It is expected to be about 8,500 million by 2,020. As population expands there are a number of specific environmental pressures:

- Natural resources become more heavily utilised. This may be directly, as the resources are used for living – for example wood for fuel, or indirectly, as in the use of natural resources to create wealth.
- Pressure on living space becomes greater. This may mean that marginal land is used for housing rather than agriculture. Also, there will be

pressure on other living species as humans push their own boundaries ever further.

● Land which is used for food crops will be more intensively farmed.
● Waste products will also increase, as will the need to develop an appropriate infrastructure to cope with increased population. All of this puts stress on the environment.

ii) Agricultural development

Technological advances have tripled the productivity of world cropland during this century. They have helped expand the world grain harvest from less than 400 million tons in 1900 to nearly 1.9 billion tons in 1998.

LR Brown, *State of the World*, p. 115

Modern agriculture poses problems for the environment too:

● As agriculture becomes more industrialised, the use of machinery may produce polluting side-effects.
● As more food is needed, but requires to be produced using less land, intensive agriculture practices are employed. This means that there is a greater reliance on the application of chemicals – with all the potential side-effects which that implies – in order to get the highest yield possible per acre. In the long term this may involve significant land degradation – for example desertification.
● Such intensive agriculture may also employ chemical application to make use of land which is marginal – i.e. land which has not been used previously for agricultural purposes. This land, however, may well have supported many wild species which will be lost as it is turned to agricultural use.
● Intensive agriculture also makes use of monoculture. This is where vast areas of land are used to grow single crops (and usually the same species of that crop). The problem with this is that in doing so the genetic diversity of crops is reduced and the monoculture crops are far more susceptible to disease than greater varieties of crops would be. This means that where monoculture is used as a means by which to feed the world more affordably, it might also lead to famine as monoculture crops fail.
● One way around this is the use of genetically modified (GM) crops. These are crops which have the genes of another living thing inserted artificially so that the crops adopt a certain desirable quality. For example, many fish produce natural 'anti-freeze' which allows the fish cells to survive extreme cold. If these genes were introduced into, say tomatoes, then these crops would be better able to withstand frost and so more likely to be successful. GM foods are presented by their supporters as the way to avoid world hunger, because GM foods are better able to resist failure (their assumption being that world hunger

is caused by the failure of food crops). Opponents claim that the development of GM foods is too unpredictable. They also claim that they may harm non-GM foods as genetic material is exchanged outwith the control of human hands – with unpredictable results. However, GM foods are one current approach to providing for the needs of the growing human population, and as the debate about them is still in its infancy, you should make sure that you are fully up to date about the issues surrounding it.

4 Ethical responses

... we need a new moral compass to guide us into the twenty-first century – a compass that is grounded in the principles of meeting human needs sustainably. Such an ethic of sustainability would be based on a concept of respect for future generations.

LR Brown & C Flavin, *State of the World*, p.21

a) Egoism

The egoist is unlikely to concern himself with poverty unless it is his own, or, if it is someone else's, that it might somehow affect him. An egoist may well take a 'survival of the fittest' view of national poverty. He may conclude that if you happen to live in a poor country then that might be unfortunate, but not his concern. Some have suggested that those who allow 'market forces' to control the world economy are guilty of just such an egoistic approach.

Many consider a national expression of this the practice of 'protectionism'. This is where a country introduces procedures or rules which protect their own industries from international competition, at the expense of industries abroad. Many might consider this to be an example of national egoism.

However, should the egoist be convinced that turning a blind eye to poverty might cause him harm, he may alter, if not his beliefs, then his actions. Let us say, for example, that the existence of world poverty and economic inequality is more likely to lead to a politically unstable world. This could result in wars and other forms of unrest. This could affect the egoist. In this case, it is now in his own self-interest to assist in the alleviation of poverty. Similarly, if world malnutrition is shown to lead to more worldwide disease epidemics, then the egoist would have a vested interest in helping alleviate such malnutrition.

As far as development is concerned, the egoist may only concern himself with his own country. He may be very sceptical of aid programmes, because they would appear to cost him – albeit indirectly – while not benefiting him at all. If he were an egoist living in a developed country, he may actually welcome the debt of poor countries, because it effectively subsidises his own life at others' expense. Similarly, the egoist might welcome population growth and the economic and agricultural development of developing nations, regardless of their environmental impact, if they had some direct benefit for him. For example, if the egoist were a fridge manufacturer he may welcome plans to have a fridge in each Chinese household – even though such a process may be environmentally harmful.

In short, an egoist's response to the issues involved in this chapter would vary depending upon which side of the development 'fence' he was sitting on, but always, the key feature would be his own self-interest.

b) Utilitarianism

In terms of sheer numbers, the utilitarian should be concerned with poverty. The notion that 5 per cent of the world's population controls 90 per cent of its wealth clearly is the opposite of what the utilitarian would desire. A utilitarian would therefore want to support programmes which distributed wealth more fairly. World poverty has been explained as an issue of distribution – the utilitarian would want to see wealth distributed so that the greatest number secured pleasure. Moreover, poverty's effects extend beyond those suffering it presently. It can have de-stabilising effects generally – for example in aggravating world political instability – which means that it can be considered to affect everyone. The utilitarian, John Stuart Mill noted the wider effects of poverty in 1861:

> ... no locality has a moral right to make itself a nest of pauperism, necessarily overflowing into other localities, and impairing the moral and physical condition of the whole labouring community.

Utilitarianism, p.169

In addition, the effects of poverty do not only cross national boundaries, they are long-lasting and unpredictable. This means that they have the potential to cause misery to many in the future as well as now. Clearly this does not satisfy the utilitarian's desire for the maximisation of pleasure for the greatest number.

The utilitarian would therefore support economic development where it would be likely to lead to the maximisation of happiness for the majority. This pleasure would come from the improved conditions of those living in developing countries, the greater world stability which their improvement would produce, and also the satisfaction of those in the developed world, freed from any 'guilt' that their pleasure is at the expense of the majority. However, where this economic – or agricultural – development might have significantly adverse environmental effects, the utilitarian will have to weight up the issues carefully. The improvement of life for the majority now would be less attractive if it were at the expense of far greater numbers in years to come. A utilitarian therefore, would welcome economic development, but would want to ensure that such development was undertaken in a sustainable way so that the benefits for future generations were maintained.

c) Altruism

The altruist would want to alleviate poverty for the benefit of others. Also, the altruist would be prepared to make any necessary self-sacrifice in order to bring this about. Most of us act in an altruistic way when we give to charities or support overseas aid. The altruist, however, would argue that governments should behave in a systematically altruistic way. The issue for a government, however, would be in whose interests they ultimately act. Clearly national governments do not wish to diminish the standards of living of their own populations, but if they are to act altruistically towards developing nations, then to a certain extent that may be inevitable. Many countries have cut their overseas aid programmes, though many argue that they have done so in order to protect the development of their own country. There is always a tension in any government between alleviating poverty in their own land and helping other nations. For example, in the USA, there are many pockets of very serious poverty, and yet the USA is looked to, as one of the world's wealthiest countries, to give a lead in alleviating world poverty. The altruist personally is presented with a challenge in relation to the balance between helping the poor who are 'close' and those who are far away – but help he must.

As far as development is concerned, the altruist would want there to be a systematic approach taken which is based on concern for others. This approach can take any form, but might be less likely to support tied aid because this could be seen as replacing one burden with another. Again, however, the altruist would want to be assured that any development undertaken by developing nations was not likely to be so environmentally harmful that the drawbacks ultimately outweighed the benefits. For example, should a dam project help a country industrialise, it should still be questioned where it results in painful social upheaval. The altruist, like others, would want to ensure balance – in this case, that the benefits for others were clear and realisable and not outweighed by any negative effects generally.

d) Situation ethics

Here, poverty's causes and effects will have to be dealt with as they arise. If a certain action is likely to lead to poverty then it should be examined as to its positive and negative outcomes. The difficulty with situation ethics – for the poor – is that there is no absolute value given to one state over another. In other words, the situation ethicist has no absolute priority for the alleviation of poverty as against the creation of wealth. Governments would find it difficult to approach poverty in this way (though many might claim that they do), because they have to take an approach which generally gives priority to one over the other. Even where a government gave a high priority to alleviating poverty, it might abandon this entirely should some other pressure come along. For example, in times of war or as the result of natural disasters, a country may end completely programmes which aim to alleviate poverty – either in their own country or overseas in order to cope with the more immediate situation. Similarly, while a government may generally support overseas aid, it may withdraw it where the recipient country falls from favour. Also, a country may block aid, or cease trading with another country whose politics it disagrees with, thus worsening poverty for those in that country. For example, Iraq has recently experienced trade embargos because of political disputes. It is often argued that the only ones to suffer from this are the poor. While governments and individuals probably do act as situation ethicists often, this is usually a detour from their usual, more systematic approaches.

Similarly, in relation to development. The complexity of the world economy makes a situation ethics approach both more likely and perhaps less satisfactory – at least for the developing nations. Take for example, trade: while a developed nation may take the general approach that trade with developing nations should be fair, where situations preclude such fairness, the developed nations may 'change the rules'. For example, a developed nation undergoing an economic slump of its own may seek to reduce its spending on imports. Developing nations may find themselves unable to sell their goods – or having to sell them for very little (either that or not sell them at all). Thus, in response to a situation outside their control, the ethical rules have altered to the detriment of the developing nations. Organisations such as Traidcraft seek to behave in such a way as to even out these anomalies, by ensuring that developing nations enjoy consistent rewards for their efforts irrespective of the variations in the world economy.

The situation ethicist rarely works in a moral vacuum. It is more usual that those who employ situation ethics may have some general principles which themselves may be altered in response to specific situations. However, as an ethical approach to development issues, it probably leaves a lot to be desired.

e) Legalism

Poverty itself is not illegal; neither is causing someone to be poor. Certain 'unfair' practices which result in poverty are legal, and others are not. The definition, legally, of what is reasonable and unreasonable in relation to causing poverty is vague at best. Governments have legal obligations to provide as best they can for their own people – and ensure that poverty is minimised. There are absolute standards which are enshrined in a country's laws. However, the complexity of poverty's causes means that legal force cannot easily be brought to bear – either on governments or individuals. There are some instances – for example, in the UK the introduction of a legally binding minimum wage means that employers have an absolute duty to reward someone's work at a set minimum level. Also, in Britain at least, equality of opportunity is supported by the law, so that if you are economically disadvantaged by belonging to any social or ethnic group, that can be legally challenged. However, other instances of poverty are less clear. It would be extremely difficult for someone poor to prove that any individual or government was legally responsible for their misfortune. In relation to world poverty this is even more complex. The amount of aid that may be given to the world's poor nations is subject to no law, nor any legal enforcement. Moral obligations are quite different from legal ones. The legalist therefore is on shifting sands in relation to the alleviation of poverty. All that he can hope to do is to firm up the law with respect to preventing poverty and supporting those who might experience it. He may like, for example, to see overseas aid become the subject of international law rather than simply international agreement.

Likewise, there are no laws about developed nations assisting the economic or agricultural growth of developing ones. The exploitation of individuals or countries could well be the subject of legal proceedings under a human rights banner, but this would be extremely difficult to pursue. For example, while a British company may be required to pay a minimum wage to workers in Britain, no such requirement might be in force should that company choose to employ workers in a foreign country, where local laws will apply. This means that such a firm could significantly cut its labour costs while able to act outside the legal restrictions of the country in which it is based. Similarly, the environmental impact of development is subject only to international agreement, not law. It would be a legal minefield for anyone wishing to prove that a country's development involved environmental side-effects which could be considered worthy of criminal or civil proceedings.

f) Religious authority

Many religions differ about the underlying causes of poverty:

- Some Jews, Christians and Muslims might take the view that poverty is a sign of God's disfavour. The poor are in some way being punished for their actions. Or they may consider poverty to be some kind of moral test – to see whether the afflicted person remains faithful to God despite the adverse circumstances in which they find themselves.

● Or they might argue that poverty is another of the symptoms of mankind's arrogance, a direct result of selfishness and the rejection of God. The drive towards material success leads to a society which cares less for those who are in poverty. Though this view is more widespread, it does not follow from it that the poor should be abandoned.

● Eastern religions might argue that poverty is the result of bad actions in a previous life. Hinduism, Buddhism and Sikhism believe in reincarnation. They believe that throughout your life, your actions create the 'blueprint' for your personal nature. Your rebirth is therefore a direct consequence of how you behave. This could mean that the poor could be seen to be suffering misfortune as a result of their own bad actions. However, this does not mean that nothing should be done to help them.

Most religious groups focus a considerable amount of their time and energy on the alleviation of local poverty, and many run substantial programmes of aid to developing nations. Organisations such as Christian Aid are active in helping the poor. This action is motivated by their belief that in helping the poor they allow the teachings of Jesus to be seen in action, as well as by the idea that every person reflects God in his life. Christians believe that humans are made in the image of God. Mother Teresa of Calcutta claimed that she saw Jesus in the poor and that is what motivated her to help them.

Christian responses have tended to focus more on responding to the effects of poverty, and less on the underlying causes. Liberation Theology, however, has been instrumental in challenging the world structures which maintain divisions between rich and poor. Unfortunately, such theology has often been criticised, not only by world governments, but by those within the Christian faith itself. Many take the view that religion and politics should be kept separate, while many others regard this as an impossible division. At any rate, when religious groups have made comments about the causes of poverty, they have often been effectively told to keep out of what does not concern them:

> When I feed the poor they call me a saint, when I ask why they are poor they call me a communist.

> Dom Helder Camerra

Whatever the causes of poverty may be, Christians take the view that it is a duty and a moral obligation to lessen its impact as far as possible. This may be by direct action, or by influencing those in power to do what is right. Christians tend to take the view that poverty is intrinsically wrong, regardless of its causes, and that it demonstrates a failure of mankind to treat each other fairly.

Similarly, in Buddhism, the emphasis is on making sure that the person is fed and nourished properly, because without that there is no hope that the person will be able to listen to Buddhist teachings. The Buddha himself is reported to have refused to teach people until their physical needs were provided for. The implication being that the teaching of a faith will be of little value if people remain hungry, and so the first priority is ensuring that poverty is alleviated.

Development too, for the Christian should be a moral obligation. The idea that all are equal in the eyes of God is expressed in Paul's letter to the Galatians. No one should be disadvantaged in relation to others. That is not to say that there will not be those who are better off than others, simply that everyone should expect the opportunity to prosper. The economic and practical disadvantages of being born into a developing nation should not preclude you from having the same life chances as one who is born into a developed one. The Jubilee 2000 campaign – inspired by Christian groups – takes just such a view. It argues that the debt of developing nations should be cancelled. The motivation for this is simply that it provides an 'even playing field'. The removal of the obstacle of debt means that developing nations will be in a position of equal opportunity, and better able to develop having had the crippling debt burden removed.

It is claimed that Jesus had a 'bias towards the poor' – his teaching was aimed at putting right social as well as spiritual wrongs, and he seemed to see wealth as an obstacle to spiritual progress. The importance of providing for life's physical needs comes through in Gospel stories such as the 'Feeding of the Five Thousand'. Jesus, like Buddha, seems to have taken the view that material provision is necessary for spiritual enlightenment.

In Eastern religions, the obligation to assist is also present. It would be difficult to support the view that a developing nation was experiencing its difficulties because of some collective accumulation of bad karma. However, it would be possible to argue that not to support the development of these nations would give rise to further bad karma. Therefore, the obligation to assist a developing nation improve the lot of its population is clear whatever religious tradition you follow.

5 Conclusion

- The causes and effects of poverty are complex.
- Most ethical traditions recognise the need to alleviate poverty where possible.
- Economic injustice in the world has complex causes and not always clear solutions. However, almost all ethical traditions would support action which might lead to a fairer world, though their motivation might differ.

- Economic and agricultural development are complex issues with specific environmental implications.
- The growing human population presents significant economic, agricultural and environmental challenges.

Study guides

Summary List

You should build your study notes on the following:

- To what extent does interaction within human society pose environmental problems?
- What are the likely causes and effects of poverty, and what ethical issues does its existence raise?
- What is the relationship between the developed and the developing world, and what issues does this raise?
- To what extent is there economic justice in the world?
- What practical and ethical issues are raised by international debt?
- What are the advantages and disadvantages of aid programmes?
- To what extent is economic development desirable and achievable?
- What issues are raised by industrialisation and agricultural development, and what are their environmental implications?
- What are the causes of and possible solutions to world hunger?
- How do various ethical traditions respond to these issues?

Examination Guide

Questions in this area are likely to ask you to do the following:

- demonstrate knowledge and understanding of the issues involved in poverty, development, economic justice, hunger, and international relations between the developed and developing world.
- show how these issues raise ethical problems and be able to outline how various ethical traditions might comment upon them.
- show that you are aware of the ways in which human interaction in the world raises environmental issues, as well as issues of equality, fairness, justice and the like.
- demonstrate that you are aware of the complexity of the issues involved, but that you can support a reasoned conclusion on any of the topics studied.

Sample Essay Question and Guide

'The cancelling of debt repayments for the developing world is economically naive.'

How might someone who follows ONE of the ethical traditions you have studied respond?

1. Choose which ethical tradition you will use as the basis for your answer.
2. 'Unpack' the question by showing that you understand the terms involved. You may like briefly to explore what might be meant by 'economically naive', as well as set out the arguments for and against the cancelling of debt repayment. For example:

For:
- helps developing nations start off on a level playing field.
- therefore allows them to shake off dependence upon developed nations.
- may therefore result in wider social improvements in developing nations as side-effects of economic development.
- results in global economic justice, which may make the world a more politically stable place.
- may benefit developed nations, as economically independent countries will be in a better position to engage in real trade with them.

Against:
- may harm the economies of developed nations.
- may provoke global economic instability.
- developing nations once developed may take 'revenge' on those who subjugated them for so long, thus it could ultimately lead to global political instability.
- removes the dependence of developing nations on developed ones, therefore developed nations will see their power decrease.
- any benefits may not reach the people they are intended for.

3. You may like for each of these, or at least for a few of them, to make some comment about how the follower of the ethical tradition you have chosen might respond.
4. As you raise each element of the issue, you should ensure that you evaluate the implications with reference to the ethical tradition you have chosen. For example:

… the cancellation of debt repayment would also allow developing nations to free themselves from being dependent on the developed world. An altruist would agree that this was a valuable outcome, because it means that others benefit even if some – in the developed world in this case – may have to make sacrifices. Of course, the sacrifices which may have to be made are not at all of the same order as the benefits which will be produced, so the altruist will be able to support the mild discomfort of others in the developed world for the greater benefit of the real advantages which might be had by those in the developing world. For someone in the developed world it might mean fewer luxuries, for someone in the developing world, a few more necessities. This, the altruist could justify …

5. Remember to include a reasoned conclusion, supported where possible by hard facts and figures as well as supported argument. The implication of this question is that the person making the statement thinks that naive = wrong. It is up to you to show how far this is true in relation to the ethical tradition you have chosen.

Typical Examination Questions

1. To what extent can the interaction of humans be considered an environmental issue?
2. 'The poor shall always be with you' Mark 14:7, Christian Bible. To what extent do you agree?
3. How far might an egoist support the cancellation of international debt?
4. 'Aid programmes from the developed nations are often ethically dubious.' Discuss.
5. To what extent might a utilitarian support industrialisation in a developing nation?
6. 'World hunger is the greatest threat to the environment which mankind presents.' To what extent do you agree?
7. 'The job of religions is to feed the spirit, not to feed the hungry.' How might a religious person respond to this statement?

Activities

This section lends itself well to outside speakers, as well as to events. Most of those involved in work with the poor and in assisting developing nations have fairly detailed programmes of education and publicity. There are also many organisations which will be glad to enlighten you about their work. Also, this section covers numerous issues which fall into the political arena, and so you should aim to find out more from local politicians at a variety of levels and of all shades of the political spectrum. Again informal and formal debates are of value here, as well as specific tasks – for example devising programmes for use in your own educational setting which will inform others about what you have been studying. Many people who begin studying this area of ethics find that it becomes a major feature of their lives. Certainly, the more most people find out about poverty, the more they want to do something about it.

Suggestions for Further Reading

1. *Environment, Population & Development*: P Sarre (Ed), Hodder & Stoughton, 1991, ISBN 0 340 53360 9
2. *The Third World Atlas*: The Open University Press, 1990, ISBN 0 335 10259 X
3. *Is That It?*: Bob Geldof; Penguin, 1986, ISBN 0 14 009363 X
4. *Comfortable Compassion*: C Elliot, Hodder & Stoughton, 1987, ISBN 0 340 40737 9
5. *A Vision of Hope*: United Nations Report, 1995, ISBN 0 95204695 4
6. *Eliminating World Poverty: A Challenge for the 21st Century*: UK Government white paper, HMSO, 1998
7. *State of the World 1999*: LR Brown & C Flavin (Eds), Earthscan, 1999, ISBN 1 85383 594 3

5 Conclusions

> **KEY ISSUES**
> - To what extent is the world on which we live in a state which should concern us?
> - What is the role played by humans in relation to the rest of the natural world?
> - What predictions – about the issues we have explored in this book – can reasonably be made about the future?
> - In what ways can the human species corporately and individually respond to environmental issues, and to what extent should we?
> - What role can be played by ethics in all of this?

1 The state of the Earth

The Worldwatch Institute's special millenium publication, *The State of the World 1999*, makes the following observations about the current state of the environment in 1998:

- the first eight months were the warmest of any comparable period on record.
- China's Yangtze river had its worst flood for 44 years.
- Bangladesh experienced its worst flooding since records began.
- in Honduras, 70 per cent of the country's crops were washed away by Hurricane Mitch
- 3,000 people died in India's worst heatwave for 50 years.
- some 45 countries were stricken by severe droughts.

It concludes:

> Such trends show clearly that from an environmental standpoint, we are not ending the century on a bright note. (p.xix)

The United Nations report, *A Vision of Hope*, outlined the 'Human Development Balance sheet' for 1995:

- while most countries in the developed world provide for their populations well, there are still instances where, 'poverty is still very much in evidence despite the overall abundance of society at large'.
- despite increased wealth in these developed nations, and the freedom it brings, 'this freedom has a high price – individual trauma, the disruption of children's lives and family impoverishment. Crime and misbehaviour are rising as the signs of personal distress appear more manifest'.
- in developing countries much is left to be done to improve quality of life and, 'economic progress itself is not a straightforward matter nor an uninterrupted push forward'.

It concludes:

> It is ironic that environmental degradation is usually caused by affluence in the North and by poverty in the South. But it would be quite unfair if global limits were imposed on the South's development in a manner that limited its potential. The world will have to find a way to share the same environmental space in an equitable manner. (p.137)

As far as the animal world is concerned:

- many more people reject inhumane treatment of animals, as well as the use of animals for products which are considered luxuries.
- renewed emphasis is placed on trying to find alternatives to the use of animals for medical and scientific research, and many countries have significantly tightened their laws in this respect.
- However, many species remain endangered, and there are areas in the world where the treatment of animals has not improved significantly if at all.
- In 1999 *New Scientist* magazine carried out a major survey into people's attitudes towards the use of animals for experimental purposes. It reported considerable confusion among the public about views held. It appeared that attitudes changed depending upon the phrasing of the question.

One of the conclusions of this survey was:

> There is a gap in people's knowledge. No prescription drug is marketed without first being tested on animals, yet people are either unaware that this is the case, or don't want to acknowledge the fact.

> *New Scientist*, 22 May 1999, p.30

While there may be disagreements about the fine detail of the state of the Earth today, there is agreement that we need to keep a watchful eye on environmental issues. Although there are those who criticise the current emphasis on environmental damage as 'doomsayers', even they do not suggest that we close our eyes and hope that it all somehow goes away. It is probably accurate to claim that everyone involved in environmental debate has a vested interest – their own axe to grind – but it would be wrong to dismiss everything that is said because of that. Someone's motivation for raising or muting the environmental alarm may be suspect, but that is not the same as saying that they are wrong.

Humans have a unique ability to understand the world in which we live. To fail to make use of that ability would not be wise.

2 What of the future?

Assuming that few people in possession of their faculties would wish to close their eyes to actual and potential environmental change, various options are open to us should we wish to tackle environmental issues:

- adapt to the changes as they happen. This may involve rapid change and sudden diversification. It could be unstable and impractical. Due to the unpredictable nature of environmental change it could be difficult. However, it needs little or no forward planning, and sacrifices need only be made in response to an actual and not a perceived situation. However, it would probably require an element of stiff coercion when necessary.
- prepare for the changes in advance. This might be difficult however, as the changes could be so unpredictable.
- prevent the problems which are expected to arise before they do. This will take significant legislation or social coercion, and may involve sacrifices being made by some for the benefit of others, with no directly perceived benefits now.
- All of these approaches could involve a social, economic, political or technological response.

The difficulty is that there is no absolute guarantee that anything we do will improve the potential situation, nor that anything we don't do will worsen it. However, we do have to act in a way which takes account of the best possible advice that we have at any one time, otherwise we might as well bury our heads in the sand. Every action we take will have an element of unpredictability, but few would agree that this should preclude us from acting at all. Imagine those who had opposed child slavery in the UK in the past had refused to act for fear of unpredictable consequences.

What is required in all of the environmental debates is open-mindedness on all sides. Each side needs to be able to understand the viewpoint of the other – even if they don't agree with it. Perhaps therefore, the greatest environmental threat today is ignorance.

3 Making a difference

> For our discussion is on no trifling matter, but on the right way to conduct our lives.
>
> Plato, *Republic*, VIII, 352d

This book began by stating that environmental issues are complex. You should now be better aware of that complexity and better able to understand and analyse it. Views about the issues you have studied vary widely. Moreover, they are often contradictory and may involve significant conflict. Depending upon what you read, and how you interpret what you read, you may conclude that:

- The Earth, and life on it is in a precarious state. Living things and natural systems are so finely balanced that the scales could tip at any moment resulting in environmental catastrophe.
- Though finely balanced, nature has its own ways of ensuring stability. The balance will be achieved without human intervention – perhaps even despite it.
- Nature works on the basis of long time-scales. What appears to us a crisis is just a natural part of a normal cycle of events.
- The Earth has its own rights.
- The Earth is there to be plundered in order to improve our own lives.
- Human interaction on Earth is unfair and likely to lead to social and political chaos. We should examine carefully how we treat others.
- Human interaction on Earth is just natural competition where the strong survive and the weak do not. It should be allowed to take its course, even if that appears to be harsh.
- Industrialisation and technology are the keys to environmental improvement.
- A return to a simpler, pre-industrial state of living is the key to environmental improvement.
- Animals exist for human use and so how they are treated by us is irrelevant.
- Animals have their own rights, and deserve reasonable treatment.
- No matter how much we know and what we do, the human species cannot effect environmental change on purpose.
- By study, research, examination and exploration of the issues involved humanity can make a difference.

This book has aimed to explore the issues without taking sides. However, one thing is certain. In this case, ignorance is most certainly not bliss.

The fundamental capacity of humans to be self-aware, self critical and understand their actions – as well as predict the likely outcomes of their actions – is crucial. The philosopher Plato said, 'the unexamined life is not worth living' (*Apology* 38a). In many respects that is what this book has been about. Your choosing to study these issues is a mark of your having decided to examine your own life and the lives of those around you. We can extend Plato's statement to include society generally, because what is the value of human society if it does not exercise its unique ability to examine itself?

The issues may well be complex, there may not be any immediately obvious answers, but the effort to understand should continue. If there is an environmental crisis, then how that came about and what to do about it should be an urgent focus of our attention – without which our physical survival may be imperiled. If there is no environmental crisis, then that same process of examining our relationship with nature, other life-forms, and each other should continue – if for no other reason than to ensure that problems do not creep into existence unnoticed. We depend upon the Earth, and much of the life on it, for our continued survival. Everyone has a vested interest in ensuring that the environment remains 'healthy'.

> The philosophers have only interpreted the world in various ways; the point is to change it.
>
> Karl Marx, *Theses on Feuerbach*, (1888), xi

There would be little point in simply studying these issues if such study did not lead to action. The environment is not a museum, it is a living system. Whatever we do has effects. We should study these effects and then act upon our findings. Even if we find that we need do nothing now, if we do not maintain the examination, then we won't necessarily know when to cease our inactivity.

Most philosophers would agree that philosophy – particularly ethics – should guide our daily lives. Whenever we make a decision (and doing nothing is also a decision) we should make sure that we are as well-informed as possible and have thought through the issues as carefully as we can. Being aware of the ethical issues surrounding a topic, as well as understanding a variety of responses to these issues, helps clarify our own thinking. Clear thinking is usually the best foundation for considered action. Having studied environmental ethics you will now be in a better position to do something about the issues – where you judge that something needs to be done.

Change is a feature of life on Earth, and for humans, such change is most often a direct result of self-examination. For example, many oil companies are now spending very large sums of money exploring sustainable energy – like solar energy. These companies currently depend upon oil for their existence, but their assessment of future trends in the supply of and demand for energy has led them to dip their toe in unfamiliar waters. This reaction is a direct result of both scientific assessments and gaging public perceptions of energy production methods – it therefore has a practical and an ethical dimension. Organisations such as Fair Trade report booming business, as people reflect on the cost to developing nations of the current economic system and vote with their wallets. The UK has seen a great deal of debate recently about hunting, and it is rare to see a fur coat worn in public these days. It is clear that, as far as the issues which this book has explored are concerned, people are thinking very carefully about their relationship with nature, and changing their lifestyles accordingly.

4 What now?

> ... few of us spend much time wondering why Nature is the way it is; where the cosmos came from, or whether it was always here ... every now and then I'm lucky enough to teach a kindergarten or [primary

school] class ... they're curious ... provocative and insightful questions bubble out of them ... they've never heard of the notion of a '[stupid] question'. But when I talk to [secondary school pupils] I find something different. They memorise 'facts'. By and large, though, the joy of discovery, the life beyond those facts has gone out of them. They've lost much of the wonder ... they're worried about asking '[stupid] questions'; they're willing to accept inadequate answers ...

Carl Sagan, The Demon-Haunted World, p.301

Ethics should challenge. You have explored the science, the economics, the politics of environmental issues. Now you should interpret them ethically. You have been exposed to the general principles of a variety of ethical traditions, as well as the ways in which these respond specifically to the environmental issues examined in this book. The question should now be; 'What do I think?'.

You may have begun your study with set views – perhaps firmly held views, or you may have begun not knowing what to think about this complicated area. Whatever the case, the hope is that you now build upon what you have learned and ask questions of it. There is little point in simply learning, repeating and forgetting. Education should be more than that. The issues which you have studied affect us all to some extent – so you should have a view on them, and be aware of the views of others, even if you disagree fiercely with them. The poet, Goethe said, 'he who cannot draw on three thousand years is living from hand to mouth', by which he meant that the pupil should build upon the learning of others – and eventually become more knowledgeable than the teacher. This book is aimed at students studying A-level courses. In a few short years your generation will be responsible for the world in which we live. It would be nice to think that when that happens, your education has enabled you to exercise your responsibilities well. HG Wells supported the value of education about the environment when he commented that, 'human history becomes more and more a race between education and catastrophe'.

Life on Earth is involved in a constant struggle for survival. Inevitably this involves competition. It is just this competition and conflict which is the source of many of the environmental issues we have explored. The scientist Carl Sagan suggested:

Let us compete ... in eliminating government corruption; in making most of the world agriculturally self-sufficient. Let us vie in art and science, in music and literature, in technological innovation. Let us have an honesty race. Let us compete in relieving suffering and ignorance and disease; in respecting national independence world-wide; in formulating and implementing an ethic for responsible stewardship of our planet.

Carl Sagan, Billions and Billions, p.163

By all means compete to get the best possible grades for your exams, but learn as well.

Study guides

Summary List

You should build your study notes on the following:

- To what extent can the environment be considered to be in a 'healthy' state today?
- Why is it important to maintain an interest in environmental issues?
- What possible options are open to us in terms of responding to environmental issues in the future?
- What role does ethical reflection play in understanding and responding to environmental issues?
- How have your own views changed through your study of this area?

Examination Guide

There may well be questions in your exam of a more abstract theoretical nature. These questions will be specifically designed to focus particularly on your evaluation and analysis skills. They will expect you to synthesize information and use such information to support arguments of a more abstract and theoretical kind. Such questions will expect you to use the informational aspects of environmental issues to illustrate more general ethical points. You may also be asked questions here which ask you to engage in much more speculative thinking, for example, to consider the likely consequences of one course of action or another. In answering these you should be able to demonstrate that you have command of the material, and that you are able to use it to support your own developing environmental ethic.

Sample Essay Question and Guide

'Concern for environmental issues is not just practicality, it's part of what makes us human'.
To what extent do you agree?

1. This question asks you to weigh up the reasons why, if at all, humans should be concerned about the environment. The aim is to compare and contrast functional reasons for being concerned with more abstract, yet equally important ones.
2. You could perhaps begin by giving a brief outline of current environmental concerns. But don't get carried away, this is not a descriptive answer, it is an evaluative one.

3. Then show in what ways it is a *practical* issue i.e.:
   ● the issues have implications for our lives, in that if we spoil the environment we may have to suffer the negative consequences of that action.
   ● our existence as a species has significant impact on the environment which cannot be ignored.
   ● only humans have the ability to alter the environment to any great extent, and so practically we must examine how that is and should be done or limited.
4. Given that this is a more theoretical question, you should probably focus on the second element concerning 'what makes us human'. Even if you don't agree, the question requires that you outline the argument:
   ● humans have a unique ability to reflect on their actions. They should therefore do so.
   ● ethical thinking is a unique human function, it should therefore be employed here because:
   − environmental issues are not just issues of science, politics or economics; they are also issues of belief. Your philosophy of environmental issues will guide your actions, and being human, it should.
   − humanity's role on Earth implies responsibility. Such responsibility implies that we continually examine the implications for nature of the very existence of the human species.
5. Your conclusion should take one side or the other. It is likely that having studied this course (and not simply a course in environmental science), that you think there is a significant role for ethical reflection in this area. Perhaps therefore your conclusion could look something like this:

The philosopher Plato reminds us that, 'the unexamined life is not worth living'. As far as we know, humans have a unique ability to reflect on their beliefs and the actions which those beliefs lead to. What we think about the value of the environment, about the living things which are part of it − and about the other humans with whom we share the world − will affect the choices we make. Failure to reflect ethically on these issues is not only practically inappropriate, it is also denying the very things which make us human ...

Typical Examination Questions

1. To what extent is the environment in crisis?
2. 'Humans should be concerned only with their own kind.' How far would you agree?
3. How far would you agree that the best approach to environmental problems is to deal with them when they take effect?
4. 'Technology is the key to putting right our environmental mistakes.' How far would you agree?

5. 'The study of, and responses to, environmental issues should be left to the scientists and the politicians.' To what extent do you think such an attitude is reasonable?
6. How far is education about environmental issues vital to the development of human society?

Activities

This short chapter has encouraged you to synthesize materials already learned. At this stage you will be going over much of what you have previously studied and reminding yourself of the ethical dimensions to it. You should take the opportunity to test yourself in a variety of ways, as well as use some of the exam questions throughout the book to devise your own exam paper which you should aim to do in the time which will be available in the actual exam. It is also a helpful activity to read others' exam answers, and to mark them as if you were the teacher. This will help you to see where marks are allocated, and how others structure work, as well as reinforcing the basic ideas of the course.

You should also consider perhaps the most important question of all: 'What do I do now?'

Index